W9-ASC-260

MAKING
THE MOST
OF YOUR
MIND

MAKING THE MOST OF YOUR MIND

by
Stephen B. Douglass
and
Lee Roddy

CAMPUS CRUSADE FOR CHRIST
Published by
HERE'S LIFE PUBLISHERS, INC.
San Bernardino, California 92402

MAKING THE MOST OF YOUR MIND
by Stephen B. Douglass and Lee Roddy

A Campus Crusade for Christ book
published by
HERE'S LIFE PUBLISHERS, INC.
P.O. Box 1576
San Bernardino, CA 92402

Library of Congress Catalog Card No. 80-70022
ISBN 0-86605-109-0
HLP Product No. 40-088-7
© 1983, Stephen B. Douglass and Lee Roddy

All rights reserved.

Manufactured in the United States of America.

FOR MORE INFORMATION, WRITE:

L.I.F.E. — P. O. Box A399, Sydney South 2000, Australia
Campus Crusade for Christ of Canada — Box 368, Abbottsford, B.C., V25 4N9, Canada
Campus Crusade for Christ — 103 Friar Street, Reading RGI IEP, Berkshire, England
Campus Crusade for Christ — 28 Westmoreland St., Dublin 2, Ireland
Lay Institute for Evangelism — P. O. Box 8786, Auckland 3, New Zealand
Life Ministry — P. O. Box/Bus 91015, Auckland Park 2006, Republic of So. Africa
Campus Crusade for Christ Int'l. — Arrowhead Springs, San Bernardino, CA 92414, U.S.A.

TO JUDY

Contents

Foreword

I have known Steve Douglass and Lee Roddy for many years. What especially causes me to recommend this book to you is that they are well qualified to write on the subject and they practice what they write.

Steve graduated number one in his high school class of 400 and went to the Massachusetts Institute of Technology to study electrical engineering. He went from there to the Harvard Graduate School of Business Administration and graduated in the top two percent of his class. In his ministry career with Campus Crusade for Christ, he has been called upon constantly to use his mind in planning, organizing, leading, speaking, writing and teaching. Steve has been one of the greatest challenges to me in these areas.

Lee's entire career has evolved around using his mind to communicate to people. He has been a newspaper reporter, feature writer, columnist, editor and publisher. He has written or edited for more than 50 national or international Christian organizations and leaders. He has been a Hollywood radio dramatist and motion picture and television writer. Lee in one word is "creative."

Not only are they qualified, but they obviously have worked hard to create a very helpful book for you. If you have any interest in making the most of your mind as God intended, you will want to read it. I know of no other book like it. It details how to improve in a wide range of mental attitudes and skills. It contains proven, practical, easily applied and well-illustrated material. Most important it shows you how to use your mind to tap into the infinite wisdom and power of God.

Whether you are a student, homemaker, professor, truck driver or executive, you will benefit from this book. Who doesn't want to make the most of his or her mind? Who doesn't want to make better decisions, have better attitudes, be more creative, communicate more clearly, or remember more effectively?

I highly recommend that you read this book and apply it to your mind. I have desired to use my mind extensively through the years. I have had to learn these principles the hard way. My growth in mental attitudes and skills could have been greatly accelerated had I been able to study this material earlier in my life.

Making the Most of Your Mind is a "must" book for any Christian.

Josh McDowell
Julian, California

Acknowledgments

We want to express sincere appreciation to the following people for their part in this book:

Steve's wife, Judy, for her active mind, constant encouragement and joyful willingness to allow time for her husband's writing.

Michelle Preston, for her many overtime hours of typing done with enthusiasm despite the pressure of a publishing deadline.

Rosalie McMaster and Ann Smith, for their careful, quality research.

Anne Nelson and Dr. Dennis E. Hensley, for their skillful editing.

Jayne Cole, Pat Sanchez, Kirk Joseph and Yvonne Clapper, for their typing at the early stages of the book.

Ron Jenson and Larry Poland, for their stimulating, creative ideas.

Lloyd and Laura Copenbarger, for the use of their mountain home at a key point in the writing.

Albino Hinojosa, for his art work, which makes the message clearer and more easily remembered.

1

GETTING STARTED

There is a man who is an outstanding scholar, powerful speaker, inspiring leader and insightful advisor. However, his wife has found that he often forgets very important information she has told him. One evening, for example, he was babysitting with their children. When she came home, she found he had not remembered to give the children their supper.

She has learned that if she really wants to be sure he remembers something, she has to work at it. She grabs him by the ears, brings his face next to hers and says, "Watch my lips and repeat after me. . ."

Do you ever have problems remembering things? Do you find it difficult to think because of pressures you face? Do you often feel you can't follow the reasoning of another person? Do you have trouble making decisions or thinking of creative solutions to problems? Have you ever found it difficult to explain what you mean?

If you said "yes" to any of these questions, and want some practical help, then this book is for you.

William James, about the turn of the century, was a Harvard professor and one of America's leading philosophers and psychologists. He observed, "Compared to what we ought to be, we are only half awake. Our fires are dampened, our drafts are checked. We are making use of only a small part of our mental and physical resources."[1]

James believed that the average man utilized only 10 percent of his mental capacity. The great scientist Albert Einstein felt the ratio was even smaller; he believed we use only five percent of our minds.

It has been demonstrated through scientific research that children learn about 25 times more per day than adults do.

If you feel you are using only a small fraction of your mental capacity but would like to increase your ability, this book will show you how.

In the first chapter of Joshua, God commissioned him commander-in-chief and spiritual leader of the children of Israel. In verse 8, God says, "This book of the law shall not depart from your mouth, but you shall meditate on it day and night, so that you may be careful to do according to all that is written in it; for then you will make your way prosperous, and then you will have success."

Note how God emphasized the need for Joshua to be mentally disciplined through reading, studying and meditating. Joshua was placed in a position of leadership, but with this appointment came the responsibility to acquire wisdom and mental order. Similar admonitions are also found in the New Testament.

In Romans 12 we find the apostle Paul exhorting the Roman Christians concerning Christian living and service. In verse 2 Paul declares, "And do not be conformed to this world, but be transformed by the renewing of your mind, that you may prove what the will of God is, that which is good and acceptable and perfect."

In both passages, we see that the desired end product is true success in life. In Joshua's case, this involved being a successful general and spiritual leader, conquering the land God intended for the children of Israel, and settling His people there. In the Romans passage, Paul seems to suggest that Christians can attain even God's perfect will for their lives.

In both passages we see that the mind is crucially involved. Joshua was told to meditate constantly on the law of God. The Roman Christians were told to renew their minds in order to gain a transformation into a new and better life.

Do you sometimes find yourself thinking about things that seem to drag you down mentally and emotionally? Do you find it difficult to relate the Bible to your life in the twentieth century? Is your relationship with God something less than a personal, vibrant one? Do you want to experience success in life in the most satisfying way?

If you answered "yes" to any of these questions, this book will help you. It is about your mind and how to use it well. Here's what you will learn:

1. How to become motivated to use your mind most effectively.
2. How God can relate to your mind and cause you to make the most of it.
3. How to use simple, specific and practical techniques to improve your mental skills.
4. How to apply what you learn to your daily life.

The Miraculous Mind

The human brain, the mind, is one of God's most amazing creations. Medically, this three-pound collection of matter has 30 billion nerve cells and approximately 300 billion glial cells. The brain makes up only two percent of body weight, yet it demands 20 percent of the blood pumped through the body and a similar percentage of the oxygen taken into the lungs.

The brain is the recorder of every memory and the seat of every sensation gathered by the five senses.

There are two levels to the brain: the conscious and the subconscious. The first has familiar functions, whereas the latter controls automatic breathing and heartbeat (even while asleep), and subconscious learning and analysis.

The brain works somewhat like a computer, although it is superior in many ways. Like a computer, the brain will act upon what has been put into it. What we think about tends to determine what we do and what we become. Proverbs 23:7 states, "For as he thinks within himself, so he is."

Research has shown that after three repetitions of the same act a habit begins to form in our subconscious mind. For example, as an infant, Steve's daughter Debbie learned to grasp things with her hands. The first several times it took her total concentration to accomplish this feat. Then, slowly, a habit was formed. Before two months passed, she could grab a pen out of Steve's pocket while he was lifting her up from the floor. The details of grasping had become a habit for her.

William James observed:

> Sow an action and you reap a habit;
> Sow a habit and you reap a character;
> Sow a character and you reap a destiny.[2]

God has given human beings incredible potential. He has given us guidelines for wise living, far beyond the wisdom of our limited experience. "The testimony of the Lord is sure, making wise the simple" (Psalm 19:76). What we do with our minds is no casual matter.

God promises us great benefits if we live according to the wisdom that He has given us. For example, it says in Proverbs, "My son, do not forget my teaching, but let your heart keep my commandments; for length of days and years of life, and peace they will add to you" (Proverbs 3:1-2).

In the same chapter we also read, "How blessed is the man who finds wisdom, and the man who gains understanding. For its profit is better than the profit of silver, and its gain than fine gold. She is more precious than jewels; and nothing you desire compares with her. Long life is in her right hand; in her left hand are riches and honor. Her ways are pleasant ways, and her paths are peace. She is a tree of life to those who take hold of her, and happy are all who hold her fast" (Proverbs 3:13-18).

If we can learn to harness the potential of our minds, we can live life at the best possible level—where God intended us to live when He created us. But if we open our minds to just any influence, however bad, and fail to learn to utilize our mind's potential, we sentence ourselves to mediocrity or worse.

For example, Lee had striven to become a writer for more than 40 years without much success. All this time he had sought to do this with his own strength. He read books on how to succeed, but success eluded him. Then he learned that God had a purpose for his life—that He believed in him and wanted him to be a writer for His glory. Without fully realizing it, Lee began to follow some of the principles shared in this book. During the next eight years, he wrote and sold 30 books, five of which later were made into films and three of which were rated best sellers. Why? God showed him how to make more effective use of his mind.

In recent years, a number of secular books have related success to the power of the mind. The authors of these books have begun to plumb the depths of the reservoir of potential God has placed in the human mind.

Napoleon Hill was one such secular writer. He interviewed 500 of the most successful men in America, including such magnates as Henry Ford, John D. Rockefeller and Thomas A. Edison. Hill sought the secrets of their success. After 20 years of research he wrote an eight-volume omnibus called *The Law of Success*, parts of which are condensed in his best-selling book, *Think and Grow Rich*. Hill concluded that among the crucial ingredients to success were (1) a burning desire, (2) a definite purpose, (3) unwavering persistence and (4) a constant mental focus.[3] It was the mind in each of these four findings that had made the successful person become successful.

Hill later co-authored the book *Success Through a Positive Mental Attitude* with W. Clement Stone, a Christian businessman. As you might imagine, the central ingredient to success mentioned in this book was the maintenance of a positive mental attitude. The authors stated, "A negative mental attitude is one of the primary causes of failure."[4]

God placed these success capabilities in people's minds. As the capabilities are tapped, people achieve significant accomplishments. Even more—much more—can be accomplished as they are tapped in the context of a close relationship with God.

Overall more scientific progress has been made in the last half-century than was made in the previous thousand years. This fact can be best exemplified by thinking of the advances in flight. In 1903 the Wright brothers flew the first airplane for 12 seconds at 31 mph for a distance of 852 feet. By 1969 man had landed on the moon. Such amazing progress baffles the imagination. Similarly, a 1908 Ford Model T had a four-cylinder engine which could run up to 27 mph. In 1982 the contestants at the "Indianapolis 500" qualified for entry at speeds beyond 200 mph. These are only samples of recent accomplishments. The technology which made such things possible was conceived by the brain. Theoretically, it was possible to have done these things generations ago. But it was the unfettered minds of more recent persons that achieved the seemingly impossible.

Of course, significant accomplishments have been made in past centuries, too. The Great Wall of China and the pyramids of Egypt still cause us to marvel. By the grace of God, these amazing feats were conceived first in the minds of men, who envisioned them, believed in them, and then made the dreams become realities. But in each case, it was the minds of a few individuals — unrestrained by the usual standards of thought — which contributed most to the accomplishments.

Some minds are always active. They appreciate the ideas generated by other thinkers. James D. Newton, a modest, quiet man of great spiritual faith, was a personal friend of such renowned thinkers as Thomas Edison, Charles A. Lindberg, Henry Ford, Harvey Firestone and laureate Dr. Alexis Carrel.

Mr. Newton says these men had several things in common. They had the ability to keep things simple, to think a problem through, and to persevere until what their minds had envisioned became reality.

The human mind is somewhat the same in every human being, but what is done with that mind depends upon the individual.

Rochunga Pudaite, now president of Bibles of the World, was born in an East Indian village hut of the tribe called Hmar, former headhunters of Maniput territory of northeast India. When he was nine years old, alone, barefooted, he walked 96 miles through the Indian jungles to gain an education so he could translate the Bible into his tribal tongue. He worked his way through college in order to complete his original project. Then, he went on to develop the idea of putting a Bible into the hands of every person listed in the world's telephone books.

Being a jungle-born boy wasn't a handicap, for God had given Mr. Pudaite a mind which could match that of any man who had been born in the West. Mr. Pudaite used his God-given mind well.

Unfortunately, as we have already learned, most of us waste 90 percent or more of our individual mental capacity. But we don't have to! Intensified mental focus under God's direction can achieve great things. Consider this: diffused light will reflect harmlessly off a wall, but when that same light is focused intensely enough to become a laser, it can cut right through that wall.

If you desire to learn how to focus your mental power to laser-like intensity, read on.

In this book, we will offer you positive steps which you can take to move toward pushing your mental capacity to its highest and best use. We hope to motivate you to take those steps.

Attitudes and Skills

What you are about to learn can be summarized this way: For your mind to function at its best, certain fundamental *attitudes* must be formed and certain *skills* must be developed.

A few years ago *Parade* magazine ran an article about champion athletes in many sports. The article declared that "mental attitude, not physical ability, is the prime ingredient of a champion." The article added, "The difference between winning and losing, success and failure, is in the mind and not the muscles." Key attitudes include mental peace (being free from anxiety), teachability, inquisitiveness, motivation, positiveness, discipline, persistence and flexibility of pace and focus.

The right attitudes applied over a period of time led to the development of skill in these athletes. No basketball player, for example, can become successful if he doesn't have the mental confidence in himself which spurs him on to practice and become skilled at shooting baskets. So mental attitude is very important.

Then we must add refined mental skills to right attitudes if we

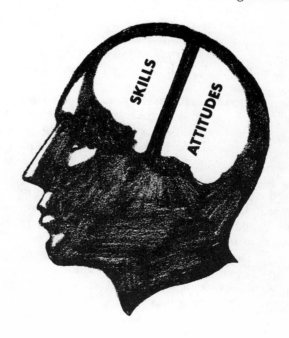

are to make the most of our minds. Key mental skills include observing, interpreting and organizing thoughts, listening, reading, studying, being creative, planning, solving problems, making decisions, remembering, speaking, and writing.

In the following chapters you will learn how to develop these key attitudes and skills.

Be forewarned, however: if you read a hundred books on this subject and had perfect recall of them all, you would still find it impossible to make the most of your mind if you did not seek the supernatural wisdom and power of God. He is the only Being with a mind capable of dealing with infinite complexity. He can discern what is going on in the mind of the person to whom you are talking, and keep you from saying the wrong thing. God knows the future. He knows perfectly the outcomes of alternative courses of action, and He can keep you from making the wrong decision. God can give you the wisdom to look at an overwhelming number of facts, discern which are relevant to your situation and to judge properly how to interpret them. God is the only being capable of freeing your mind from anxiety in a painful, even impossible, situation.

Therefore, without apology—in fact, of necessity—we focus on how to establish and maintain a kind of personal walk with God that truly will enable you to make the most of your mind. In this book, you will learn how to pray and study the Scriptures for wisdom and how to walk closely with God in your mind, as well as in your actions.

Since God has graciously given us such a wonderful gift as the mind, the least we can do is be good stewards of it. Although 1 Peter 4:10 refers specifically to spiritual gifts, the principle also could apply to the gift of the mind: "As each one has received a special gift, employ it in serving one another, as good stewards of the manifold grace of God."

The mind is the key human ingredient for spiritual growth and true success in life. However, the average person uses only a small fraction of his mental capacity and does not seek to draw wisdom from God, who offers it without reproach (James 1:5).

The choice is yours. If you want to continue achieving only part of what you are capable of, stop here. If you want to learn to harness and sharpen your mind, proceed.

We are not content to have you simply read. Research has shown that people learn much more by *doing* than by just reading. So, at the end of each chapter, we will offer you some ways to make greater use of this book and of your mind.

You will discover a Personal Application Worksheet at the end of the book. At the end of each chapter you will be asked to think back over what you have learned and then to write in this worksheet the point from the·chapter which is most applicable to you at this time. We will also ask you to take a moment to write down a few thoughts on how you can begin to implement this point into your life. This will greatly increase your learning and personal benefit from the book. We want you to be able to make better use of your mind right away.

Additionally, you'll find three other items at the end of each chapter:

1. Thought questions which will help you think through topics in the chapter;
2. An action project which will call for you to learn by doing something; and
3. A reminder to look at the Further Study Materials section at the end of the book for additional information on the subject covered in each chapter.

According to your time and interest in a given chapter, you will want to take advantage of these special features.

— — —

I. PERSONAL APPLICATION

What is your highest personal priority application from this chapter? Is it "believing that you can use more of your mind"? Perhaps you were particularly struck by some fact or quote or passage of Scripture. Whatever it is for you, write it down in the indicated column and the row on the left side of the worksheet. Next, write down a specific plan to start implementing this application point. It might involve reading more in this book. It might involve studying more, doing something, sharing ideas with someone, or praying. Whatever it is for you, write it in the indicated column and row on the right of the worksheet.

II. THOUGHT QUESTIONS

Think through the answers to each of these questions. Discuss them with a friend, if possible.

1. What do I think is a fair estimate of how well I use my brain? If I were called upon today to give an account to God of the stewardship of my mind, what do I think He would say to me in response?
2. What specifically would I like to do better with my mind if I could? What benefits would there be for me and others?
3. Romans 12:2 says, "be transformed by the renewing of your mind." Specifically how does that work?

III. ACTION PROJECT

It is the authors' intention that the Action Project at the end of each chapter will greatly increase the book's effectiveness because you will be requested to take an action and not simply think about what's just been presented. This assignment is designed to make the concept *yours*.

The following is the assignment for this chapter. Improve your mental attitude about some person you don't like by doing this exercise:

1. Write down as many good characteristics as possible about that person.
2. Daily meditate on those characteristics.
3. Before you see that person, make sure you've decided to mention one of those positive attributes to him or her.
4. Do this for a week and see how you feel about that person. Compare the difference in a week or two.

IV. FURTHER STUDY MATERIALS

For more information on getting started, you will want to consider the Further Study Materials for this chapter listed at the end of the book.

HANDLING ANXIETY AND GUILT

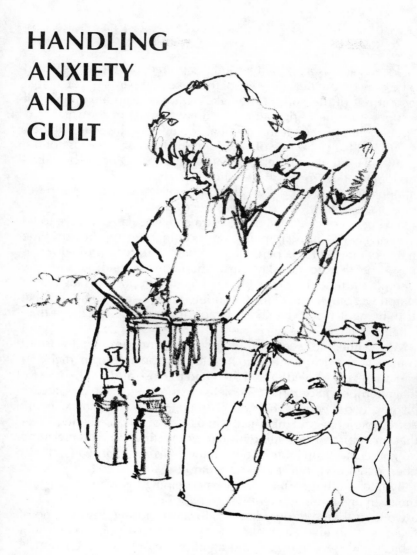

2

Early on the morning of February 28, 1978, Steve was putting on his jogging outfit. His mind drifted to his father who was in the hospital with a problem that had yet to be diagnosed. His father had been living with Steve and Judy, and she had taken him to the hospital the day before.

On his way out of the house, as Steve passed through the kitchen he saw ants crawling on the cake his wife had made for that evening. The cake was for some special friends who were coming.

He looked at the cake carefully and discovered that the ants seemed to be only on the outside edge of the cake and pan. He cut a large section out of the core of the cake, wrapped it in aluminum foil and put it in the refrigerator. He threw the rest of the cake out.

When he returned from running, Steve found his wife lying on the bed with a pulse rate of 120, suffering from an overdose of the spray she used to treat her asthmatic condition. Quickly, he called the emergency room in the hospital. It turned out that the epinephrine in the spray would simply wear off after a period of time. No trip to the hospital was necessary.

Having to cope with all of the extra activities caused Steve to be late for his first appointment that morning. He teaches on time management and it is particularly anxiety-producing to show up late, especially to the day's first appointment. Shortly after the meeting started, one of the top leaders of Campus Crusade called him. It was very difficult for him not to take the call so he did take it, thinking it would be short. Unfortunately, it lasted more than a half hour.

Meanwhile, the meeting rumbled on behind him, but it was not coming to a conclusion. When he returned, the meeting participants had a brief time together and then had to close and reschedule for that afternoon in order to complete the meeting. Steve was late for his next two meetings. He and his secretary covered some urgent correspondence and then he dashed to a luncheon meeting. After that, he returned to resume his earlier meeting. By mid-afternoon he got to the hospital to see his father. His problem had still not been diagnosed, but it looked ominous.

By late afternoon Steve was home helping his wife prepare for the evening's entertainment. Their friends came over and they had a wonderful time during dinner. However, during dessert, one of the guests observed a single ant crawling across the dining room table. Only Steve knew the full significance of that ant. Obviously not all of the ants had been on the outside edge of the cake. The diners had consumed more "nourishment" than they had realized during dessert.

During dinner Steve received a phone call from a person who wanted to stop by to deliver something after the other guests had left. At 10 o'clock he came by and dropped off the item.

About 10:30 he finally had a chance to call his father to see if he had learned any more. His words burned into Steve's mind. "Son," he said, "I am afraid they have discovered that I have terminal cancer."

That was a day filled with situations which produced anxiety. Things didn't work according to plan. He was late. There were embarrassing moments for him. There were pressures from other people. And he learned that someone he loved was seriously ill.

Can you identify with this day? Gratefully, not every day is that bad. Yet, almost every day has some sources of anxiety and if we do not deal well with them we will not function well during the day.

Anxiety Hurts

Anxiety is one of the great detractors from our ability to use our minds to their maximum levels of effectiveness. It is difficult to focus on how to make a wise decision, how to remember something, or how to find the cause of a problem if our minds are filled with other thoughts. This problem is compounded if these thoughts are emotion-laden concerns. They constantly grab our attention away from whatever else we are trying to think about. We will never make the most of our minds if we are distracted by anxiety and don't learn to deal with it.

In the New Testament *merimnao* is a Greek word frequently translated as "be anxious." The word literally means "to have a distracting care." One example of its use is found in Philippians 4:6 where it says, "Be anxious for nothing, but in everything by prayer and supplication with thanksgiving let your requests be made known to God." Here we are told not to have a distracting care about anything, but instead to deal with it.

There are many things that can distract our minds. For example, when we sin and feel guilty afterward, we have caused anxiety. In Psalm 38:18b we find, "I am full of anxiety because of my sin."

Causes of Anxiety

Many times the various things we want and need in life can cause anxiety. This is especially true if they are not present in sufficient supply. If we lack food, clothing, potential length of life or purpose in life, we find ourselves becoming anxious. But Jesus tells us not to be anxious (Matthew 6:24-34).

Sometimes circumstances cause anxiety. A man who was waiting in the subway for his train stood at the edge of the concrete platform where he expected the car to pull up and the doors to open. He was wearing a brand new suit and tie and was admiring how good he looked in them.

Unknown to him, a man in the approaching train was late in delivering two pies. The delivery man had to exit at the very stop where the first man was waiting. As the train slowed to stop and the doors opened, the person in the train jumped out. He collided with the waiting man and smashed the pies all over the man's new suit.

Horror stricken, the delivery man stepped backward. Before he realized that he was back in the subway car, the car doors closed and the train pulled away. The first man stood at the edge of the platform, looking down at his suit and saying, "Why me, Lord? Why, me? And I don't even *like* lemon pie."

Unfortunately you can't always avoid bad circumstances. Sometimes you just find yourself caught up in them. You must learn how to deal with them. For whatever the cause of anxiety, and however it occurs, our minds are certainly not going to function at the level God intended unless we are able to deal with that anxiety.

How to Handle Anxiety

We have found three steps which can be taken to reduce anxiety. There are many specific techniques that could be mentioned under each step. The three steps are:
  1. Eliminate the cause.
  2. Displace the thoughts.
  3. Treat the symptoms.
The rest of the chapter gives some detail regarding each of these main points.

1. ELIMINATE THE CAUSE.

One of the best ways to eliminate the cause is to solve whatever the problem is. For example, when a speaker goes to a speaking engagement, he could easily worry over whether or not an overhead projector and overhead projector pens will be available. The easiest way to solve that problem is either to ask specifically that they be provided or to bring them along himself. Once the problem is solved he doesn't have to think about it anymore.

Sometimes people will lie awake at night wondering if they left a light on or an air conditioner running in the living room. The easiest remedy is to check to see if there is a problem. If there is, simply correct it.

Some people find a need to carry this technique a little far. In his book, *Secrets of Mind Power*, Harry Lorayne tells of a man who worried about having an appendicitis attack while he was on a business trip. The man worried about the business he would lose if this happened. He also worried about having to have an operation by a strange doctor in a strange city.

Logically, the odds were very small that the man would ever have had such an attack. But it was such a concern that he had his own doctor remove the appendix during an off season on his job. After that he didn't have to worry about an appendicitis attack.

Dealing with Guilt

Another common way to eliminate the cause of our anxiety is to confess our sin. If we have sinned, the guilt we feel becomes a cause for anxiety. The only legitimate way to eliminate the feeling of guilt is to confess the sin. In John 1:9 we read, "If we confess our sins, He is faithful and righteous to forgive us our sins and to cleanse us from all unrighteousness."

In Psalm 32:5 David tells us, "I acknowledged my sin to Thee, and my iniquity I did not hide; I said, 'I will confess my transgressions to the Lord,' and Thou didst forgive the guilt of my sin."

In addition to confessing our sins to God, at times we need to confess our sins to others whom we have wronged. This is not easy. But if we don't, we will probably find recurrent feelings of guilt plaguing our minds. This is probably God's Spirit telling us to do something about it.

One time Steve was in a small Bible study on James 3 being conducted by a friend of his. The topic related to the controlling of the tongue. When it came time for discussion, the group became fairly informal and humorous. In that context he made an indirect reference that could easily have been interpreted as being critical of the leader. The remark was funny; the group context was informal; and the remark was not directly critical.

Despite all this, Steve felt a pang of guilt concerning what he had said. No matter how he sought to rationalize it, he felt guilty. He confessed his sin to God, but he still felt the need to seek the leader's forgiveness. He didn't want to say anything in front of the group, because supposedly he should have been one of the more spiritually mature members of the group. He even had a chance to get out of saying something, since there was a phone call for him just before the end of the discussion time. However, he decided to return that person's call later, drew a deep breath and asked the leader for forgiveness for his critical remark. He did forgive him. From that very moment Steve experienced a clear conscience from the matter. That was one less thing that could nag on his mind thereafter.

If you make this your practice, you will be able to say with Paul, "Brethren, I have lived my life with a perfectly good conscience for God up to this day" (Acts 23:1).

Cast Your Cares

Another very significant method for eliminating the cause is to cast cares on God. In 1 Peter 5:7 we read, "Casting all your anxiety upon Him, because He cares for you." When we cast our cares on God it means we are trusting Him to solve the problems and to take away our concern for them. That does not mean we may not be a part of the solutions to the problems; it does mean that God takes away our distractions.

A few days after Steve learned of his father's imminent death, the real impact of it hit him. He was seeking to take a nap on a Sunday afternoon when he found tears welling up in his eyes because he would really miss his dad. For two hours he cast that care on God. Slowly but surely he sensed the burden of it shifting from him to God. Thereafter, he still experienced concerns related to his father's problem, but the burden had shifted to God. Many times we give lip service to our trusting God, but often we are not willing truly to trust Him.

The story is told of a man who was doing a tight rope act over Niagara Falls. He first walked back and forth a few times. Then he took an empty wheelbarrow with a special grooved tire on it and went back and forth. Next he filled the wheelbarrow with about 200 pounds of weight and went back and forth. When he returned to the side where the audience was watching everyone cheered. He asked how many people believed that he could take a loaded wheelbarrow all the way across Niagara Falls and back again. All raised their hands. The man pointed to a person in the front row and said, "Great! Why don't you hop in and let's try it?" The spectator replied, "Oh, no! I don't *really* believe you can do it."

That's the way a lot of us are. How about you? When you face a situation of anxiety and you pray and ask God to take it, do you trust that He will take it? If He—through His Word or in other ways— gives advice as to what to do, do you take the advice? If you don't, you are not really trusting.

For people who tend to feel things quickly and deeply, learning to cast cares on the Lord is especially important. One Christian lady we know tends to see things readily that aren't as they should be. She will often feel strongly that change should occur. These are wonderful qualities of life in terms of internal motivation to cause positive change. Unfortunately, these strong feelings can easily turn into anxiety. She has had to learn to cast her cares on the Lord quickly and completely or she will suffer.

Before you read the next section of this chapter, pause for a moment and consider the things that are causing you to have anxiety right now. Look over the ways we have shared with you as to how you can eliminate the cause of anxiety. Can any of them apply to your particular situation? Pause, pray, think, and then apply. Then read on. At the chapter's end, we will refer you to the Personal Application Worksheet.

2. DISPLACE THE THOUGHTS.

Sometimes we can't eliminate the cause of the anxiety. We are forced to face it on a constant basis. Yet, at times, we are able to displace the thoughts of it. Right now, try not to think about a chocolate milk shake. Try not to think how tall and delicious and cool and attractive-looking that would be. (If you like some other flavor, try not to think about that instead of chocolate.) The harder you try not to think of it, the harder it is for you not to get that image in your mind. As a matter of discipline, it is difficult to remove that image. But it is possible to remove it by causing yourself to think of something else. The key, of course is to think about or focus on the right alternative things.

Focus on God

How do we do it? First and most important, is to focus on God. That is one of the most successful techniques we have found in eliminating the thoughts of anxiety in our hearts and minds.

In Matthew 6:33 we read, "But seek first His Kingdom and His righteousness; and all these things shall be added to you." In Colossians 3:1-3 we find, "If then you have been raised up with Christ, keep seeking the things above, where Christ is, seated at the right hand of God. Set your mind on the things above, not on the things that are on earth. For you have died and your life is hidden with Christ in God."

As we focus on God and the things of God — to quote the hymn — "the things of earth will grow strangely dim, in the light of His glory and grace."

One time a young man was eating lunch with a friend of his when the friend's wife joined them. The only seat available was the one to the left of the young man. So she took that seat. After lunch, she came back to the seat with a styrofoam cup filled with hot water for tea. She placed the tea bag and the stirrer in the cup and set everything down at the right of her tray. As she talked she turned to say something to the young man and knocked over the cup. The

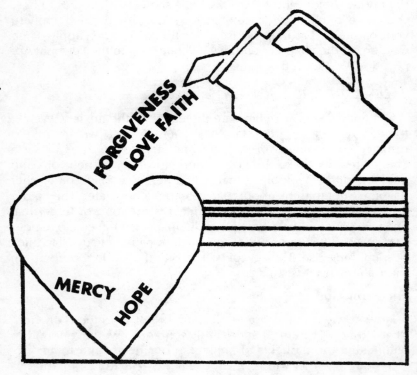

entire cup of fresh hot tea spilled onto his leg without spilling a drop on her.

The young man learned two things from that experience. The first was that you should not sit next to someone else's wife; you could get burned! The second, and more serious lesson, came from his reaction to the incident. He laughed instead of saying, "Ouch!" It didn't seem to hurt as much as it should have.

If you're thinking that is not normal, you're right: it isn't normal. But, you see, the young man had just been practicing what we have been talking about here. He had been talking to God while he was talking to them. And the things of earth (including the burn to his leg) had grown strangely dim.

Similarly, the things that cause anxiety in your life can become much less potent and much less dominant in your mind—if you are focusing on God in an ongoing way.

Focus on God's Word

A second, although similar, technique is to focus on the Word of God. In Psalm 1:1-3 we find, "How blessed is the man who does not walk in the counsel of the wicked, nor stand in the path of sinners, nor sit in the seat of scoffers! But his delight is in the law of the Lord, and in His law he meditates day and night. And he will be like a tree firmly planted by streams of water, which yields its fruit in its season, and its leaf does not wither; and in whatever he does, he prospers."

As we focus on the Word of God and let it fill our minds, it cleanses us of alternative thoughts, many of which cause anxiety. Especially during times of stress you will find it is helpful to read or listen constantly to the Scriptures. When you get up in the morning, listen to Scriptures on your tape recorder. As an alternative, you might put some Scripture-oriented music on the tape. Your mind will become filled with God and the things of God. That tends to displace your alternative thoughts and, as a result, what you hear directly makes you happier and more joyful.

Think About Other Positive Things

As a third thought on this subject, think about (and do) other good, positive things. In Philippians 4:8 we read, "Finally, brethren, whatever is true, whatever is honorable, whatever is right, whatever is pure, whatever is lovely, whatever is of good repute, if there is any excellence and if anything worthy of praise, let your mind dwell on these things."

Not too long ago, a prospective father attended natural childbirth classes with his wife. They studied the LaMaze method. Some of their friends used the Bradley method. In both cases distraction is one of the main methods used to keep childbirth pain from becoming unbearable. In the Bradley method, the husband's duties include whispering sweet nothings into the ear of his wife as she is experiencing pain. The idea is that she will think of him and other thoughts instead of the pain.

Some people's favorite part of the newspaper is the cartoon section. Much as it is important for people to know what is going on all over the world, the news usually does not minister to the mind in a positive way. Typically, the news is negative. On the other hand, cartoons seem to lift people's spirits, and therefore actually create a positive effect for the day.

As you engage in activities, find good aspects of those activities to think about. Be positive. Some people too often think negatively.

Shortly after Lee made a commitment to Christ, he wrote in the front of his Bible, "I have resolved that—if I know the will of God—I will do it." But almost immediately he ran into an old problem. Something didn't go well. Instantly, his old negative habit of looking at the dark side took over. In those days he was always looking for a dark cloud on which to hang his silver lining.

Yet, a glance at the front of his Bible reminded him how wrong he was to be so negative. His "belly-aching" was, to be blunt, sin. The Bible said so. "Your grumblings are. . .against the Lord" (Exodus 16:8). Therefore, it is against God's will to complain. The choice was his, so Lee decided to develop a positive voice in the unpleasant situation.

Today he may not be an overly "positive thinker," but his attitude is so changed that he can't think of anyone who has thought of him as negative in many years. Yet the choices come again and again as situations arise in which he can either trust God with positive expectations or be negative.

Some people just tend to be negative. Perhaps you have heard the definition of a pessimist? He is the person who wakes up on Monday morning and is immediately filled with anxiety over the fact that it is two days until Wednesday and he hasn't gotten anything done yet this week. He is the one who reads a book on positive thinking and now he is sure he is going to fail.

Work Toward a Solution

Sometimes it is helpful simply to work toward a solution. A few years ago there was a fire at Arrowhead Springs, headquarters for Campus Crusade for Christ. One of the best cures for the anxiety the residents and staff felt after the fire was for them to get involved in cleaning up.

Before you go on to the next section in this chapter, look back over the points we have mentioned. Are there some that would be particularly helpful to you in a situation you face? Can you turn your focus elsewhere—on God and His Word and other positive good things—as an alternative to focusing on the problem? If you can, you will doubtless experience the displacement that we have talked about and have much greater peace and freedom from your anxiety. Remember, anxiety is so prevalent you can't overdo applications to cope with it.

3. TREAT THE SYMPTOMS.

In some cases we can't seem to eliminate the cause of anxiety and we can't seem to get it out of our minds. The first two techniques haven't worked. Now what do we do? At this point it is good at least to alleviate ourselves of the disabling symptoms of anxiety.

One good way to start this process is by learning to understand anxiety. How does it happen to you? How can you avoid it? And how have you found ways to deal with it? Just understanding the material in this chapter can, in and of itself, help reduce anxiety.

Keep Things in Perspective

One good way to treat symptoms of anxiety is to keep things in perspective. This point has many dimensions. For example, a first perspective is to recognize the positive results of the situation that is causing your anxiety. Sometimes your life can be changed dramatically with the ultimate result being something positive. We are told in the Scriptures that trials or tribulations are to lead to patience and proven character in our lives (Romans 5:3-5, James 1:2-4). Thank God for the positive things He is working into your life as a result of these trials. Even if you can't think of positive things, it is good to thank God – by faith – for the anxiety.

A second perspective is to realize that God is in control. He does love us and does have knowledge of all things. These are reassuring facts when it comes to handling anxiety. What is happening to us is not out of God's view. He must have an overall purpose in what is occurring that is beyond our understanding. We can count on that as we trust and worship Him.

A third perspective is to be gained when we determine how bad our situation really is. There are some people who worry about whether or not they will sleep through the alarm clock going off. They worry so much they don't sleep in the earlier part of the night. When they finally fall into a deep slumber, they do sleep through their alarm clock s ring. Probably the best thing for them is to think through how bad it would be if they did sleep through their alarm. They might arrive a little late at work. Probably most people would not be fired for doing that once or twice. They might have to move a little faster in the morning. All in all, it is not necessarily that bad under normal circumstances. It is good to keep our perspective on what is occurring.

A fourth perspective to have concerns time. Matthew 6:34 suggests that there are enough cares for each day for us to worry about. It is scripturally out of bounds for us to worry about concerns for another day. However, many of us do not settle for simply one day's concerns. We go back into the past and get concerned about things that have already occurred or we look to the future and start becoming concerned about what could happen to us then.

Our lives could be characterized as an overloaded pickup truck, moving all the family furniture. You may have seen one of these on the highway with ropes thrown over a tremendous burgeoning overload to keep it on the vehicle. The truck rides low on the springs and the tires look almost flat. The truck, waddling down the highway, rocking to and fro, is a picture of many of our lives. We're burdened by far more than we were ever created to endure.

But if it doesn't have to do with today, we should not be distracted in our care for it. This doesn't mean we should not think ahead; it simply means we should not be distracted.

As a last perspective, sometimes it is good simply to learn to laugh at ourselves. In different surveys a sense of humor has been found to be one of the key elements of success. That's true in school, in careers and in leadership positions. Yet, many of us take ourselves too seriously. Remember, some situations are set-ups for the emotional release of humor or the emotion of anxiety. The choice is ours.

The story is told of a young man who was taking his final exam at truckdriving school. He was to respond orally to a situation the examiner would propose.

"You're driving a tractor and rig down a steep mountain road," the examiner began. "It's a two-lane road with a steep incline on your upside and a sharp drop-off to your right. As you round the curve your brakes go out. At the same moment, you see another fully-loaded truck coming up the hill in his own lane. But he is being passed by another fully-loaded truck coming toward you in your lane. Here is your final examination question: In that circumstance, what would you do?"

The young man thought a moment and then said, "I'd wake up Leroy!"

"Who's Leroy?"

"My partner. He's from a small town and he ain't never seen an accident like this one's gonna be."

Keep Fit

Another thing that you can do to help treat the symptoms of anxiety is to keep yourself physically fit. Certain vitamins are helpful in dealing with stress (e.g., B and C). But some foods are not good for times of stress (e.g., sources of caffeine).

Probably one of the most important things to do is to get sufficient exercise. Exercise burns hormones associated with anxiety and passes them out of our system. It is important, however, as we get exercise not to cause more of a problem than we are already experiencing. A particularly good exercise does not stimulate your competitiveness, or in other ways cause you additional stress. Take golf. Perhaps you can play golf with another person without being overly competitive. But suppose you cannot actually stand some of the rigors of the game without causing anxiety. For example, if you slice into the rough on your first shot, put your second shot into the sand, blast out of that and eventually get on the green and four-putt (including missing a one-foot putt) without causing anxiety, then use golf as a good way to relax. If you cannot do that, then perhaps you should try something else.

Sleep and relaxation are additional important contributors to a peaceful mind.

Be Comforted

As a last thought on this subject, be sure to allow yourself to be comforted by other people. In 2 Corinthians 1:3-4 we read, "Blessed be the God and Father of our Lord Jesus Christ, the Father of mercies and God of all comfort; who comforts us in our affliction, so that we may be able to comfort those who are in any affliction with the comfort with which we ourselves are comforted by God."

Other people can be very helpful to us in times of need. We are told in Galatians 6:2, "Bear one another's burdens, and thus fulfill the law of Christ." But many people don't like to share their burdens with anyone. If it is not necessary, and you are able to directly cast your cares on the Lord, that is wonderful. However, for many, God can use the love and concern of other people to be His tangible love to them.

Before leaving this section of the chapter, once again look over the suggested ways of treating anxiety symptoms. Are there any of these that are particularly helpful to you in situations you now face?

SUMMARY

To summarize, anxiety and guilt can come from many sources. Life is filled with anxiety causes. Our sin can cause it. Circumstances can give us grief, and other people can also do that. As a result, it is good for us not to think that we can totally avoid anxiety and guilt. Instead, we should learn how to handle them so that they are not unmanageable problems for us. In this chapter we have talked about three ways to do that:

1. Eliminate the cause.
2. Displace the thoughts.
3. Treat the symptoms.

You are never going to make the most of your mind if you cannot free your mind from the clutter of many anxieties. The ability to focus on one matter is crucial to the techniques that we will be sharing. That is why it is so very important that you learn how to handle anxiety and guilt.

I. PERSONAL APPLICATION

What is your highest personal priority application point found in the principles in this chapter? Enter that in the appropriate column and row on the Personal Application Worksheet at the back of the book. In the column next to that, enter some specific plans to start implementing that point.

II. THOUGHT QUESTIONS

1. To what extent is anxiety a mind-limiting factor in my life? Why?
2. Which of the following is most often helpful for me in dealing with anxiety?
   Eliminate the cause.
   Displace the thoughts.
   Treat the symptoms.
   Why is that?
3. Do I confess my sins to God and focus on Him often?
4. In what ways can I view my circumstances from a more positive perspective (e.g., by recognizing character development benefits from adverse circumstances)?
   Note: is there anything you want to add to your Personal Application Worksheet in light of your answers to these thought questions? Ask yourself this question after the thought questions in each of the subsequent chapters as well.

III. ACTION PROJECT

Since action should follow thought, try this: The next time you're aware of a stressful situation, specifically and consciously practice one or more of the suggestions in this chapter. Keep a record of how well each technique works for you.

IV. FURTHER STUDY MATERIALS

For more information on handling anxiety and guilt, you will want to consider the Further Study Materials for this chapter listed at the end of the book.

3

MAINTAINING THE RIGHT MENTAL ATTITUDES

Steve observed his daughter Debbie first learning to pick grapes off the little stem vines that hold the bunch together. When she saw the grapes, she was curious. She touched them. She observed her parents picking grapes off the stems. When she tentatively tried to pull one off herself, nothing happened. She pulled a little harder, but still nothing happened. Steve knew if she tugged just a little harder she would be able to pull off her first grape, but she stopped short of that. She lost interest in the grapes and moved on to other things.

Sometime later Debbie returned to the bowl of grapes. This time she had more zeal and persistence. Although she didn't pull any harder, she tried different grapes and finally she found an over-ripe one that pulled free. Once she succeeded in pulling that first grape off, she went to the next one. It was not over-ripe, but she pulled hard enough to get it off. After that, her parents had all they could do to keep the child from pulling one grape off after another. In fact, she got to where she could use both hands at the same time.

Watching Debbie learn to pull grapes off the stems was an object lesson for her dad. He saw the difference that attitude made. Her first success increased her confidence and she moved from one success to another. She even developed improved techniques to accomplish her purpose.

Had she not been inquisitive, she never would have attempted the task. Had she not tried again more persistently, she never would have succeeded. Had she not been confident after her first success, she never would have developed new techniques. She accomplished what she concentrated on.

The same principles apply to us adults. Proverbs 23:7 says, "For as he thinks within himself, so he is." In a very real sense, we become what we think. Or we can be limited by what we think.

So, in this chapter we will look at six attitudes which are key to making the most of your mind:
1. Teachability
2. Inquisitiveness
3. Motivation
4. Positiveness
5. Discipline/Persistence
6. Flexibility of Pace and Focus

As you read through explanations of each of these attitudes and see them illustrated, ask yourself whether you have enough of that attitude within yourself to make the most of your mind.

1. Teachability

Teachability requires the willingness and ability to learn. It is based on open-mindedness. In order to be teachable, we also have to be humble. An egotist who believes he is always right is not teachable.

Philippians 2:5-8 says, "Have this attitude in yourselves which was also in Christ Jesus, who, although He existed in the form of God, did not regard equality with God a thing to be grasped, but emptied Himself, taking the form of a bondservant, and being made in the likeness of men. And being found in appearance as a man, He humbled Himself by becoming obedient to the point of death, even death on a cross." Jesus modeled humility and Paul exhorted us to follow His example. That is not always easy to do. Sometimes, you really feel that you know a particular matter quite well; you feel you aren't biased, just right.

For example, a particular public speaker had that attitude with regard to a subject on which he had been teaching for many years. On one occasion a person who had heard him at a conference offered a specific suggestion. Instead of accepting his suggestion with thanks, the speaker told him several reasons why he did not teach that particular point. It was not very surprising that at the end of the conversation the man criticized the speaker's unwillingness to be open to criticism on this matter.

Later, the same speaker had a contrasting experience after he made a three-minute video tape as part of a presentation before a group of people. The next day someone suggested he could have improved his presentation by including certain things. The speaker found himself honestly interested in what this man had to say and told him so. He expressed his willingness to change his video presentation at the next opportunity. Before he left, the man commented on how open the speaker was and that he appreciated that.

It is significant that this public speaker says he cannot now even remember the suggestions the first gentleman was trying to make, but he very clearly remembers what was told to him about the later three-minute video tape. His lack of openness in the first case caused him to miss an opportunity to learn something.

In John 3 we see Nicodemus approaching Jesus to learn. This was quite a step for a Pharisee and a member of the Sanhedrin. Nicodemus was one of the few teachable Pharisees Jesus met. Part of being teachable is not blaming others for your own mistakes, but rather learning from them.

According to Lewis Timberlake, a popular motivational speaker, one of the four main reasons people fail is that they blame others for their mistakes. For example, one time a man was helping his friend paint some table legs. The table was too heavy to move outside so the friend chose to paint inside. The dilemma was that the table was on a rug which had a rather long nap, so it was difficult to keep the paint from spilling onto the rug. The friend set up the paint in such a way that it didn't seem likely to spill. After he started, however, he needed more light, so he requested a small lamp. The first man fetched a lamp and his friend set it up near where he was working. When he reached for his paintbrush, he knocked the lamp over. It knocked the can of black paint over, and it spilled all over the rug. His immediate comment was, "Why did you set things up to cause that paint spill?"

Yes, the first man certainly had brought him that lamp, but it was the friend who decided where to set it. Although both men could share the blame, the painter would have been much wiser to recognize that he had the greater responsibility for the mistake. His attitude often kept him from learning lessons that he needed to learn. Blaming others for mistakes hampers a person's teachability.

The Scriptures say, "Better is the rebuke to the wise than many lashes to the back of a fool" (Proverbs 17:10). If we are not willing to learn (whether it be by reading or by rebuke), we have cut ourselves off from the possibility of growing in knowledge.

2. Inquisitiveness

Anyone who has been around a child knows that an incessant stream of questions pours from that youngster. "Why, Daddy?" "What for, Mommy?" "How come, Grandpa?"

In a half-dozen years, a child goes from total dependency for his or her most basic needs to almost complete independence in walking, talking, speaking and planning. How? Inquisitiveness!

Children grow mentally because of inquisitiveness—they don't stop absorbing information. Neither should we.

The width of the scoop which feeds your mind is determined by your teachability. But the speed by which that scoop moves through reality is determined by your inquisitiveness. The more inquisitive you are, the more you will force-feed things into your mind. It becomes a habit.

While we usually tend to specialize our learning in the career part of our lives, we should maintain a broad interest in those things God brings our way. After all, if He allowed them to cross our paths, we should display enough continual interest to absorb information. He may well want us to know those things at a later time.

Lee has such an intensive inquisitiveness that his wife, Cicely, sometimes feels it necessary to say to people, "Don't mind his questions! He's curious about everything; that's why he's asking so many." In fact, Lee thinks one of the reasons he is a writer is because he has always been curious and has wanted to share what he has learned.

Isaac Newton is an example of a person who never lost his curiosity, and the result was a great boon to mankind. We all know the story of how he was sitting under a tree when an apple dropped on his head. That had probably happened to countless individuals before, but Newton was curious enough to try to find out why the apple had fallen. His inquisitiveness led to the discovery of God's law of gravity.

Inquisitiveness helps you function in this complex world. Hardly anything can be understood in the context of just a single discipline of knowledge. A person can have a doctor's degree in physics and still be terribly ignorant of what is going on around him unless he makes an effort to add a certain amount of breadth to his knowledge.

Make it a habit to skim a newspaper or listen to an all-news radio station daily. From time to time leaf through a magazine or book on a subject totally new to you. Occasionally participate in some new activity. All these things will give you a broader base of information from which to draw for sounder judgment and decision making and for relating better to people. This will be especially true if you will continue to ask questions as you expose yourself to new input. Paul tells us in 1 Corinthians 9:19-23 that he has become "all things to all men" so that he might fully accomplish the objective that God has given him.

When Steve went to graduate school he encountered a whole new method of learning. At Harvard Business School a system called the "case study" method was used. The students were to analyze a particular situation (or "case") and come to class prepared to discuss it with about 100 other people under the leadership of a professor. When Steve encountered this particular method of learning, he found he had to absorb knowledge in a different way. He had to ask himself questions as to what was going on and how he could best function in this new learning situation.

He observed that there were four stages to the discussion. The first was a lead-off stage. The second was what he called the reaction stage, during which people would criticize the initial presentation made in the lead-off stage. The third was the construction stage where, under the professor's guidance, everyone would seek to put together a positive solution to the case study. The fourth stage called for a summary and one or two students were given the opportunity to reflect on the case and to emphasize some of the lessons learned.

Steve quickly observed that each of these stages had far different levels of reward in terms of learning and of grades. Accordingly, he designed his strategy of study and participation in class for maximum return for his effort. Toward the end of his second year in school he was describing this system to another student. His friend acted totally amazed. It never occurred to him that was going on. In two years, this other student had never really asked himself basic questions about the course of study.

Don't let that happen to you. Learn to utilize the services of the six honest serving men mentioned in Rudyard Kipling's poem:

> I had six honest serving men,
> They taught me all I knew;
> Their names were Where, and What, and When,
> And Why, and How, and Who.

3. Motivation

The next point is motivation. The difference between an activity being fun or agony is often determined by whether or not we are internally motivated to do it.

Both authors of this book want to learn. We want to think. We have high internal motivation and energy. That makes all the difference in the world in helping us make the most of our minds. We have learned to like what we ought to do—learn. That makes it easier.

No amount of external stimulus can substitute for that genuine interest and zeal that wells up from internal motivation. It creates enthusiasm in situations which could breed discouragement. It allows for long hours to be spent on activities which would otherwise be impossible. For example, as one of your authors was writing this book, he was in a very scenic area of Colorado. During the long hours spent working on the chapters, he would look out the window and feel drawn to go out and explore. Were it not for his internal motivation to write this book, he probably would not have kept at it.

In fact, motivation is a more important quality in a person's life than discipline, in terms of follow-through on an activity. Creativity is greater when people are motivated than when they feel they *have* to do something and it is a drudgery to go through it.

The following seven techniques can increase your motivation for any project you face:

First, pray specifically that God will enable you to enjoy the project. In Philippians 2:13 we are told, "For it is God who is at work in you, both to will and to work for His good pleasure." To paraphrase a little, that means that God is able to work inside us to change our desires. He can cause us to enjoy what we thought we would not like (as long as the activity is within the boundaries of His will).

Pray and ask God to give you internal motivation and enthusiasm. God's Spirit is the energy source in the Christian life. In Acts 1:8 we read, "You shall receive power when the Holy Spirit has come upon you . . . ." So, it would be appropriate to ask God to channel that power into some particular area where we are finding it difficult to be motivated.

A Christian lecturer sometimes asks his Christian audiences, "How many of you enjoyed studying the Bible before becoming a Christian?" Not many respond. Then he asks, "How many of you enjoy studying the Bible now?" Most people respond positively to that. Why is there a difference? Because God has been working in their lives to change their desires.

In 1 Thessalonians 5:16 we are instructed to "rejoice always." Part of the natural result of living the Christian life is a feeling of joy (Galatians 5:22). God intends for us to enjoy life.

Second, keep a list before you as to why this activity is important and beneficial for you. It is very uninspiring not to know why we are doing something. Why, for example, is it important to maintain our weight at the right level? Our reasons might include: attractive appearance, good health, better mobility, good example, and longer life. A person who needs to lose weight should write these or other reasons on a piece of note paper and attach it to the refrigerator or cupboard door or both. Those are the places you need to see reminders.

You might also consider using graphic reminders. For example, suppose that having an attractive appearance is particularly motivating to some young woman needing to lose weight. She could cut from a magazine the picture of a thin model in a swim suit and place the picture on the refrigerator as a constant reminder of one benefit of losing weight. Lists and pictures can be used both as reminders and motivators.

The third idea is to find a way to do what you have to do with someone you like. A young man who was not a good student improved his grades remarkably when he started dating a young woman who was a good student. How did it happen? The woman wanted to spend a lot of time in the library. The man was unaccustomed to this, but after he had daydreamed for a while and counted the number of books on the library shelf, he finally looked down at his books to see if they had anything interesting to offer.

Steve has found this concept helpful in his exercise program. For more than two years, he had a running partner who was at the same speed and distance level as he was. They enjoyed talking together as they ran. Their friendship kept them coming out every morning rather than sleeping an extra hour. So, remember: friendship can be helpful as a motivator.

The fourth suggestion is to make a game out of what you have to do. Suppose you were offered the following exercise program: Start at one point. Take ten steps forward as fast as you can. Then take three rapid steps sideways one way, six rapid steps sideways the other way. Then return to the starting point at a walk. Now repeat the above for one hour.

No doubt you are saying, "How boring! I would never do that." Suppose you called this program "tennis"? Some of you probably already are engaged in this "boring" program. Why? Because it is an enjoyable game and the time passes quickly despite the physical exertion involved.

The fifth suggestion is for you to be enthusiastic. Part of becoming internally motivated involves learning to become enthusiastic about things. You can run without enthusiasm, but you can't win without it. According to Napoleon Hill and W. Clement Stone, "To be enthusiastic, act enthusiastic." They cite psychologist William James as their source of a proven conclusion: emotions are not immediately subject to reason, but they are always immediately subject to action. So, sing your favorite hymn of praise, or play a recording of a loud marching band, or listen to a cassette tape of a motivational speaker. Do whatever you need to do, just get yourself enthused about what you have ahead of you!

The sixth idea is to harness what motivation you already have. Some young boys flunk math but have no trouble remembering a wealth of baseball averages. Clearly they have motivation and capability in a math-related skill. It is like this with all of us. We have some things we more naturally like to do than others. Where possible, we need to find constructive ways to harness what we already like to do. For example, Steve's wife, Judy, loved to ride horses when she was a teenager. When it came time for her to get a job and earn money, one of the things she found easiest to do was to teach other people how to ride horses. That meant that she had to spend most of her day on or around horses. Naturally, that was not a tough assignment for her.

Our seventh and final suggestion is to work at staying "tuned in." Another part of our internal motivation is maintaining our alertness. Most people go through life in some sort of trance-like state. They are anything but tuned in. "Apathetic" describes many people's conditions, as opposed to motivated and interested.

To help guard against this situation in his own life, for example, Steve likes to work at a stand-up desk. When people ask him why he likes to do this his simple response is, "I have yet to fall asleep standing up." Life is too short and he has far too much to do to spend his afternoon half-dozing after a big lunch. Therefore, to stay alert and motivated he stands up or walks around in his office.

Maintaining your internal motivation at a high level is one of the most important attitudes or states of mind you can have. It will sharpen everything else you do with your mind. In many ways, it will determine your success in whatever you might endeavor to do. Abraham Lincoln was quoted as saying, "Success is going from failure to failure without losing your enthusiasm."

4. Positiveness

A former staff member of Campus Crusade, Jimmy Williams, frequently says, "You will never lead a cavalry charge if you think you look funny on a horse."

Lewis Timberlake says the number one reason people fail is that they anticipate failure. Fear is another of the top four reasons people fail. Earlier, we mentioned that Timberlake's four reasons included blaming others for our mistakes.

Norman Vincent Peale, a pastor, has spent years speaking and writing about positive thinking. He cites many examples of people who have changed their mental attitude from negative to positive and, hence have turned their lives around.

In his book, *Positive Principle*, William James declared, "The greatest discovery of my generation is that human beings can alter their lives by altering their attitudes of mind." Bob Richards, famed Olympic champion, motivational speaker, and writer, has pointed out that all champions are people who believe in themselves.

Jesus said, "All things are possible to him who believes" (Mark 9:23). And, "Be it done to you according to your faith" (Matthew 9:29).

Let us make clear that we are in no way suggesting or endorsing the idea that a person ought to substitute positiveness for trusting God, or substitute confidence in the wrong thing for confidence in what God wants him or her to do and be. What we are observing is that God placed an incredible principle in the human mind, and that if we are confident and positive and assured, God can use that to accomplish things. He uses all of the chemistry that positiveness conjures up within us to help us accomplish whatever it is that we are seeking to do. We are simply created that way. When that is coupled with God's direction, God's empowering, and God's blessing, it becomes a tremendously powerful principle in our lives.

The principle is true. The problem is getting it to work for us. It is pretty tough to fool our minds. If we know we have never succeeded in doing a particular thing, we have real doubts as to whether we have the capability to do it. We have negative, pessimistic thoughts and, partially as a result of those very thoughts, we continue to fail.

Sometimes another person can help. In order for us to get beyond our true sincere opinion of ourselves, there must be an outside influence. Sometimes another person can be this influence, but such a person is hard to find.

On the other hand, God has a perfect claim to understand us and to know us better than we know ourselves. Positive thinking is not simply a pep-talk used to fool ourselves into thinking we can do things we really doubt that we can do. It is a recognition of the fact there is a new reality about ourselves that God discloses to us in His Word. To quote a person who knew her theology better than her grammar, "God don't make no junk." God gave us dominion. He gave us the mind of Christ. We are made to succeed. So, if God thinks we can, we can!

5. Discipline/Persistence

Someone has said, "Dedication is the ability to carry out a resolution long after the mood in which it was made is gone." There are times that we do not feel motivated to continue. Yet, if our minds are put to maximum use, we must have the capability to go beyond our feelings.

There once was an advertisement for running shoes to help joggers. The ad pictured a man sitting on the side of his bed with a clock pointing to an early morning hour. The caption read, "You have to take the first step, but we can help you with the ones after that." Discipline is never easy, but it can become habit forming.

The American Management Association took a survey of top leaders to discover what qualities of leadership they might have in common. The one quality that was more common than any other was that of persistence—these people simply would not quit. They pursued and moved ahead despite resistance and, at times, often their own feelings of doubt and weariness.

It is quite inspiring to tour Thomas Edison's winter home in Fort Myers, Florida. Edison was probably the most prolific inventor of all time. A century ago, he perfected the electric incandescent light. But think of the discipline that kept him going through 1,000 or so experiments before he found the right elements. He often developed other people's experiments beyond the point where they had stopped or failed.

Edison's assistants came to him after perhaps 30,000 experiments failed to produce a battery. The assistants wanted to quit, but Edison said, "We will not quit! The answer is out there somewhere, and we'll keep searching until we find it." He did—after nearly 60,000 experiments. The result was the battery which made the submarine possible. And so Edison was able to patent many practical ideas. "But," you may say, "Edison was a genius." Well, he is the one who is credited with defining genius as "two percent inspiration and ninety-eight percent perspiration."

So, obviously, discipline and persistence are important. The question is how to obtain more of each. Fortunately for us, we can. In Galatians 5:23 we find that the ninth part of the fruit of the Spirit is self-control. The Greek word that translates as "self-control" literally means "controlling power" or the ability to be under control. As we grow and mature as Christians, this ability should characterize our lives more and more.

The question is, how can we appropriate this discipline or self-control as Christians right now? The answer is found in 1 John 5:14,15, "And this is the confidence which we have before Him, that, if we ask anything according to His will, He hears us. And if we know that He hears us in whatever we ask, we know that we have the requests which we have asked from Him."

From this verse we learn that there are two conditions which must exist in order for us to obtain our requests from the Lord. The first is that the object of our desire be consistent with God's will for our lives; the second is that we must actually take the time to ask Him for what we want, believing that He will answer our prayers.

Steve was teaching this subject in a Bible study class in which two of the members were former alcoholics. When he got to the part about the Lord supplying self-control when we cannot come up with it in our own strength, both of them nodded their heads in firm agreement. In their particular cases, the self-control was applied to abstaining from alcohol, but this same discipline can be applied to any situation where it is needed to accomplish God's will.

One successful businessman makes the claim that the best way to actually get into an activity is to begin it. He lives on Lake Michigan and has found that the only way he can start to swim in that very cold water is simply to jump in. Wading in until the water is up to his neck doesn't work. He calls his technique the "plunge" approach. God can provide the discipline needed to take the plunge into whatever it is that you must do.

"I find that I need discipline," you may admit to yourself, "to keep me going once a project is started, and particularly if it is a long one." You simply run out of gas after awhile, and an extra measure of discipline is needed to get you going again. This is particularly true of most people when a project is substantially completed, but not really done as it should be.

In order to make the most of your mind you need to be able to focus and discipline your mind and sometimes to persist in your focus over an extended period of time. Again, you can rely on the Lord to supply this discipline and persistence. Simply ask in faith, then act as evidence of your faith. "Even so faith, if it has no works, is dead, being by itself" (James 2:17).

6. Flexibility of Pace and Focus

Some of our mental activities require us to move slowly and to think carefully and to focus our attention precisely on what we are doing. Some Bible study, for example, would involve that kind of mental activity. We look at a verse and meditate on it. Maybe we memorize it. This is a slow-moving, highly focused kind of endeavor. During such times we usually avoid interruptions by working at a time and in a place where that is possible.

On the other hand, there are times when we really need to move fast, to push, to get things done. For example, in a writing project it is very important in the first draft stage not to get bogged down or overly detailed on each issue. Rather, we should link together as many of the thoughts as possible without losing momentum. It would be hard to maintain thought continuity if we got bogged down on each issue.

The problem some people have is that they are stuck at one extreme or the other. They do not have the flexibility or the willingness to move in the opposite direction.

One common reason people get stuck is they are perfectionists. This is often wasteful. "Perfectionism" is doing everything possible in regard to an item. Let's define "excellence" as fully accomplishing the function with a freedom from waste. Excellence is favorable; perfectionism can have real disadvantages. There are certainly exceptions such as artistic endeavors and things that would require great attention to detail. But for most things that we do in life, we simply need to accomplish a function. We need to fix a meal, complete a memorandum, or talk to someone on the phone. In each of these cases, we can take inordinate amounts of time if we dwell on them, focus on them and go slowly; however, it is probably not necessary under normal circumstances. Instead, we find it wiser to push through and complete what we need to do without unduly wasting our time.

Some people find that very difficult to do though. They need to remember the 80-20 rule. In most activities of life 80 percent of the good is accomplished by the first 20 percent of the time and effort, if it is the right 20 percent. Then, the remaining 80 percent of potential time and effort that you could spend on that activity would only accomplish the remaining 20 percent of the result or good.

Think of how true that is in different areas of life; for example, in a charity fund-raising event it usually is found that 80 percent of the money or even more is given by 20 percent of the people. In terms of activities in any club or church you might be associated with, 80 percent of the work is done by 20 percent of the people. Well, the principle is equally true in efforts that involve our minds. Usually 80 percent of good thinking in a subject can be done with the first 20 percent of the effort.

If you are fortunate to be in a place where the last 80 percent of the time is not needed, take advantage of that opportunity. In any case recognize the different ways that your mind needs to function for different types of activities. When you are in the early stage of a thinking process generally you need to be open, gathering facts quickly and maintaining your continuity of thought. When you are at a later stage, you need to become more analytical and critical and conclusion oriented.

Some people have the opposite problem; they have a tremendous ability to move fast and, in fact, they may be tempted to gloss over very important details. They need to learn to slow down and focus on what is called for.

The point is, you need to vary your mental pace to match the needs of what you are doing.

SUMMARY

It is crucially important that you have the right mental attitudes. Six key attitudes are:
1. Teachability
2. Inquisitiveness
3. Motivation
4. Positiveness
5. Discipline/Persistence
6. Flexibility of Pace and Focus

As you make these attitudes yours, you will be tapping into great mental resources God has given you.

— — —

I. PERSONAL APPLICATION WORKSHEET

What is your highest personal priority application as pointed out by the principles presented in this chapter? Enter that in the Personal Application Worksheet at the end of the book. In the column next to that enter some specific plans to start implementing that point.

II. THOUGHT QUESTIONS

1. What specific evidences can I give of my teachability?
2. Galatians 5:23 says that self-control is one of the essential qualities God is seeking to improve in my life as I grow in my faith. How am I growing in this area?
3. What am I already intrinsically motivated to do? How can I harness that in the most useful way?

4. Can I think of someone who tends to be negative when new ideas are proposed? What specific advice could I now give that person?

III. ACTION PROJECT

For the next few days, be as inquisitive as you can tastefully be. Ask a lot of questions. Absorb information with the enthusiasm of a child. After the experiment, evaluate how much you have learned and how your feelings have altered.

IV. FURTHER STUDY MATERIALS

For more information on maintaining right mental attitudes, you will want to consider the Further Study Materials for this chapter listed at the end of the book.

4

PRAYING FOR WISDOM

In April of 1981, Steve took a trip to Taiwan to teach management principles to pastors there. To reimburse him for his expenses, the conference sponsors paid him in traveler's checks. So, he came home from that trip with $900 in traveler's checks. There was much to do at his office, so he didn't get around to cashing the checks and replacing the money in his ministry account. Then he took another trip. When he returned, he couldn't find the traveler's checks. He looked everywhere in his office. It was quite embarrassing for the Vice President for Administration to lose $900 of his organization's money.

After several days, Steve still had not found the checks. He needed wisdom so he asked God to show him where the checks were. He remembered James 1:5 which reads, "But if any of you lacks wisdom, let him ask of God, who gives to all men generously and without reproach, and it will be given to him." One morning he hadn't had his devotions yet, but he was already in the office. God seemed to be saying to him that he should be spending some time in His Word. Steve also sensed that God was going to answer his prayer soon about the lost checks.

Steve began studying His Word. About fifteen minutes later he had the distinct impression that if he looked about three inches down from the top of a particular stack on his desk he would find the traveler's checks. He did so. There they were!

There's no doubt in his mind that God does answer prayers for wisdom.

Steve's days are almost always packed with activities which require wisdom beyond what he might reasonably expect to have in his own strength. Every meeting is begun with prayer and frequently he finds himself mentally praying on matters that are brought up in the meeting. At the end of the meeting he finds himself thanking God for the specific wisdom that He shared.

God Promises Wisdom If We Ask

This chapter's objective is to share with you how you can receive wisdom from God as promised in James 1:5. God really does want to give us wisdom and will give it to us if we ask Him for it. Proverbs 4:5 urges, "Acquire wisdom! Acquire understanding!" Matthew 7:7,8 promises, "Ask, and it shall be given to you; seek, and you shall find; knock, and it shall be opened to you. For everyone who asks receives, and he who seeks finds, and to him who knocks it shall be opened."

Clearly it is God's will that we should have wisdom and understanding along with many other good things. It is also clearly God's will that we should ask Him for things. Within the boundaries of what is good for us, it is His intention to give us those things for which we ask.

With this in mind, 1 John 5:14,15 takes on great significance when it says, "And this is the confidence which we have before Him, that, if we ask anything according to His will, He hears us. And if we know that He hears us in whatever we ask, we know that we have the requests which we have asked from Him."

Is it His will that we have wisdom and understanding? Yes! Then all we need to do is ask and we can know we have that request.

Paul gives us many illustrations which show that he believed God would give wisdom to people. One of them is found in Colossians 1:9 when it says, "For this reason also, since the day we heard of it, we have not ceased to pray for you and to ask that you may be filled with the knowledge of His will in all spiritual wisdom and understanding."

You should make it a daily part of your life to expect God to answer prayers for wisdom and provide (sometimes even in miraculous ways).

A number of years ago Steve was seeking to find a new director for the ministry of Campus Crusade for Christ called the Great Commission Foundation. He prayerfully sought such a director for 90 days without finding the right person. Then he had to move to Miami temporarily to assume the directorship himself while continuing to seek a permanent director. On the first Monday after making the move, he was in his office having his devotions early in the morning and reading John 15:7, "If you abide in Me, and My words abide in you, ask whatever you wish, and it shall be done for you."

Immediately he "heard" an almost audible voice within him saying, "Do you believe that verse?" He said, "Yes." The impression continued, "Ask that you have your director by Friday."

Steve was a little reluctant to believe that. He'd already spent 90 days seeking a director. But after a little interaction with God, he prayed that he would have the director by Friday.

Just after completing his devotions he noticed a message on the side of his desk that said he was to return a call to Warren Brock. Steve did not know who the man was, but he made the phone call. Warren indicated that a few days earlier he had resigned a position very similar to what the one at the Great Commission Foundation would be. He had heard that a director was needed and he asked that he be considered for the job.

Warren proved to be qualified and was selected as director by Friday.

How Do We Ask for Wisdom?

The following are some practical principles for acquiring the wisdom and understanding God has for us:

1. Remember that God is your Father.
2. Commit all matters to God.
3. Have faith in Him.
4. Make sure you have no unconfessed sin.
5. Keep your prayers simple.
6. Pray in Christ's name.
7. Do your part.

Let's look at each of these in more detail.

1. REMEMBER THAT GOD IS YOUR FATHER.

In the Great Commission Prayer Crusade Manual we find the quote, "Prayer is often misunderstood as a vague, mystical element in one's relationship to a holy kind of awesome God. But the Word of God does not teach this. Rather, it teaches that God, our Father, desires the fellowship of His children. Our relationship to our heavenly Father should be one of complete trust, faith and obedience."[1]

One of the most meaningful things we have discovered is the reality of God. There is a sense in which we need to relate to Him as we would relate to a person. To be sure, He is the creator of the universe, but at the same time, He has chosen to interface with us. That's basically as we would interact with people: through conversation and written communication.

What is particularly exciting, though, is that He is not like just any other person to us. He has chosen the relationship of a Father to us. That means we have certain special privileges because we are His children. In Matthew 7:9-11, Jesus made this point, "Or what man is there among you, when his son shall ask him for a loaf, will give him a stone? Or if he shall ask for a fish, he will not give him a snake, will he? If you then, being evil, know how to give good gifts to your children, how much more shall your Father who is in heaven give what is good to those who ask Him!"

One of many illustrations of God's fatherly provision occurred several years ago while Steve and his wife were traveling to Colorado. They prayed at the beginning of the trip that they would not have serious problems, that they would have a safe trip, and that the car would do well. Near Fillmore, Utah, they were getting low on gas, so they pulled off the road to buy more. The car ran best on premium gas. They went to a couple of stations which didn't have premium before finally finding one that did. This particular station was probably the biggest in town. It had the most elaborate repair facilities. They gassed up and paid for the fuel. Steve tried to start the car, but it wouldn't start. The alternator had broken. They were sitting at probably one of the only places for miles around that could immediately repair that alternator. They ate lunch while waiting for the repair to be made and then proceeded to Colorado rejoicing.

That car was an older model. It's unreasonable to assume that its parts would never wear out. But if one was going to wear out, it certainly was convenient to have it happen in the middle of a normal business day in a town and in an actual location where the repair could be made. They had no doubts God had definitely answered their prayers.

The point is that God is our Father with whom we have a relationship; He is not just a thing or a being. In prayer, remember this relationship.

2. COMMIT ALL MATTERS TO GOD.

Proverbs 3:6 reads, "In everything you do, put God first, and He will direct and crown your efforts with success" (The Living Bible). Proverbs 16:3 tells us, "Commit your works to the Lord, and your plans will be established" (NASB). The Living Bible translates that as, "Commit your work to the Lord, then it will succeed." But it's important our motives be right. If we pray with the intention to give God the glory, and not for selfish ambition, we can expect God to answer.

For example, on June 19, 1972, Lee marked the margin of his Bible, claiming Proverbs 16:3 for his career. At the time, he was a small-town newspaper editor and publisher. He wanted to stay in the field, but was convinced God was leading him into the area of writing and lecturing. At the time, he had never sold a book nor given a lecture, but, as a newly committed Christian 50 years old, he felt God's call on his life.

He sold his stock in the corporation and turned to a new field. He didn't know a single national or international Christian leader, nor the names of their ministries. Nevertheless, within two years doors had opened for him to write or edit for such leaders. He has since helped 75 well-known Christian ministries or their leaders.

By 1982, he had written, co-authored or ghosted many books, including best sellers in both the Christian and secular fields. His new books are coming out every year, mostly in the Christian field.

In 1981, he flew about 65,000 miles lecturing all over the United States and into Canada. And, he believes, the best is yet to come.

In ten years since he marked God's promise, committing his works to Him, God enabled Lee to achieve more than he had ever done before. And, on each anniversary date of that promise, something special usually happens which shows God's continuing guidance in his career. So, there is absolutely no doubt in Lee's mind that God gave him wisdom, knowledge and understanding he'd never had before he committed his work to Him. The glory belongs to God.

3. HAVE FAITH IN HIM.

We read in Mark 11:24, "Therefore I say to you, all things for which you pray and ask, believe that you have received them, and they shall be granted you." James 1:6 adds, "But let him ask in faith without any doubting, for the one who doubts is like the surf of the sea driven and tossed by the wind. For let not that man expect that he will receive anything from the Lord."

It has been said, "It is not what you pray for—but what you expect—that you receive."

The most essential prayer quality our request should have is expectancy or trust. Trust is not something we receive all at once. It grows as our relationship with God grows, over a period of time, and as we prove the truths of His Word.

Sometimes it's not easy to understand what the word "trust" means. We talked a little about that in the last chapter, but let us add another illustration. In a primitive language where the Scriptures were being translated there was no native word for trust. The people mainly had words for more tangible things, such as trees and stones. So, the translator searched and thought for a long time until finally he arrived at a good way of saying "trust" in that language.

This particular tribe used hammocks strung between two trees. The people there spent a lot of time in their hammocks. The people carefully selected the spot for a hammock. They also very carefully selected the trees to which they tied hammocks. Each tree had to bear a person's full weight so that when someone sat down on a hammock the two trees would not just bend over. There was a native word for a quality of tree that would bear a man's full weight. The translator realized that that particular word would be perfect to translate "trust" into this language. He explained, "To trust God is to put your full weight on Him, believing He will hold you up."

Honesty is the best policy with God. If you have a hard time believing God will do something for you, simply confess that to Him. Ask Him first for the faith to really believe Him, and then for the request itself.

4. MAKE SURE YOU HAVE NO UNCONFESSED SIN.

The Scriptures mention a number of things that can get get in the way of our prayers being answered. Probably the most simple summary of them is found in Psalm 66:18, which says, "If I regard wickedness in my heart, the Lord will not hear."

There are many specific sins that are listed as barriers to prayer, such as, "You husbands likewise, live with your wives in an understanding way, as with a weaker vessel, since she is a woman; and grant her honor as a fellow-heir of the grace of life, so that your prayers may not be hindered" (1 Peter 3:7). "He who turns away his ear from listening to the law, even his prayer is an abomination" (Proverbs 28:9). "You ask and do not receive, because you ask with wrong motives, so that you may spend it on your pleasures" (James 4:3).

There are also other scriptural illustrations, such as James 1:6,7, which was indicated in an earlier point.

If we find ourselves in a condition where we know we have sinned, we need to confess that sin to God. Then we can ask for what it is that He's put in our heart. Chapter 15 has more details on this.

5. KEEP YOUR PRAYERS SIMPLE.

Probably one of the most common reasons people don't pray very much is they feel a need for a special language, or a capability, in order to pray. That's really not necessary. God can hear us in any human language. He can even read our prayers of thought. It is probably best for us to tell God concisely and simply what it is that we're requesting, without needless embellishment or repetition. Jesus told us, "And when you are praying, do not use meaningless repetition, as the Gentiles do, for they suppose that they will be heard for their many words. Therefore do not be like them; for your Father knows what you need, before you ask Him" (Matthew 6:7,8).

This leads back to viewing God as our Father and not as some distant being. The more we can view ourselves in the Father-children relationship, the easier it will be to relate to Him. So, keep your prayers simple, personal, and in everyday language.

A young student's first exam in graduate school was on a math-related subject. He thought he would do relatively well on this exam since his undergraduate degree was in engineering. As it turned out, he did not do well. He was upset and had no peace. He remembered there was a verse in Galatians 5:22 which said the natural result of being a Christian was (among other things) peace. In response to that, he prayed, "God, I would really appreciate it if You would give me Your peace as promised in this verse. In Jesus' name, Amen." That's not exactly scraping the sky with theological verbiage. Yet, God immediately answered that prayer and gave the student His peace.

6. PRAY IN CHRIST'S NAME.

Jesus said, "Truly, truly, I say to you, he who believes in Me, the works that I do shall he do also; and greater works than these shall he do; because I go to the Father. And whatever you ask in My name, that will I do, that the Father may be glorified in the Son. If you ask Me anything in My name, I will do it" (John 14:12-14).

Jesus said we are to make requests to the Father in Jesus' name. Although some people may do this as a technicality, the reason behind what Jesus said is fairly obvious. Jesus enjoys a very special relationship with us. He is our Savior. He has rescued us from an eternally bad prospect. He has also provided us a very special life here on earth. As the leader of all Christians, He relates to us on a moment-by-moment basis.

Furthermore, He enjoys a very special relationship with the Father. Jesus is "His only begotten Son" (John 3:16). He also is God Himself. His special role, even now, is to intercede for us with the Father (Hebrews 7:25). In light of that, it seems natural that we go through Jesus, or at least use His name, as we make requests from the Father.

Ron Dunn, an outstanding speaker on biblical topics and a former pastor, has shared a good illustration of the better posture we enjoy with the Father as a result of Jesus' relationship with Him. One time Ron, his son, and his son's friend were at an amusement park.

Ron's custom was to hold the tickets for his son so that he wouldn't lose them.

They came to a particular ride where the son's friend had run out of his tickets. Ron's son received a ticket from his father. Then the other boy approached Ron with hand extended for a ticket.

Ron's son said, "Dad, I promised him that you'd give him a ticket." Naturally, Ron gave his son's friend a ticket because the son had offered it.

As Christians, we have a similar position with the Father because we are "friends" of His Son. So, we are able to see at least some of the reason Jesus told us to pray in His name.

7. DO YOUR PART.

Sometimes people feel that once they have asked something of God, the best thing is simply sit back, wait and do nothing while He answers their prayers. Occasionally, we find that God asks us to wait for His miraculous answer. Usually, though, it seems that He expects us to play an active part in the answered prayer. Our actions seem to be some evidence that we really believe that He is going to answer the prayer.

We must do our parts with an expectant attitude. That is part of what James 2:20 is saying: "But are you willing to recognize, you foolish fellow, that faith without works is useless?" Often we need to go forth, assuming that God is going to answer a particular prayer.

For example, if we asked for wisdom on a specific subject, we might search to see if there are sources on that topic. We can work, study hard and seek to learn things on that subject. Naturally, this is no substitute for God's supernatural bestowing of special wisdom. However, it may well be that God will reveal insight to us in the study process so we see the answer. Earl Radmacher, president of Western Conservative Baptist Seminary, once said, "God is not in the habit of blessing empty heads."

SUMMARY

In summary, God is willing to give you wisdom if you pray and ask for it. To do this you need to:

1. Remember that God is your Father.
2. Commit all matters to God.
3. Have faith.

4. Make sure you have no unconfessed sin.
5. Keep everything simple.
6. Pray in Christ's name.
7. Do your part.

As you do these things, you will experience the amazing power of prayer, available to you as a Christian:

"If any of you lacks wisdom, let him ask of God, who gives to all men generously and without reproach, and it will be given to him" (James 1:5).

"And whatever you ask in My name, that will I do, that the Father may be glorified in the Son" (John 14:13).

— — —

I. PERSONAL APPLICATION

What is your highest personal priority application point found in the principles presented in this chapter? Enter that in the Personal Application Worksheet at the end of the book. In the column next to that enter some specific plans to help you start implementing that point.

II. THOUGHT QUESTIONS

1. In five minutes how many specific prayer requests for wisdom can I list?
2. As I look·at the above summary listing of the 7 points of this chapter, can I give a brief explanation as to why each is important?
3. Do I agree or disagree with the following statement: "We need to wait for God's answer to prayer"? Why?
4. When I ask God for wisdom, why should I expect an answer?

III. ACTION PROJECT

Memorize James 1:5. Repeat it frequently during each day. Apply its promise to your daily activities.

IV. FURTHER STUDY MATERIALS

For more information on praying for wisdom, you will want to consider the Further Study Materials for this chapter listed at the end of the book.

5

OBTAINING WISDOM FROM THE SCRIPTURES

The story is told of an 80-year-old man who booked himself on a cruise of the Caribbean as a sort of last fling. The first night he was out on the deck, as were most of the other people on the boat, enjoying the beautiful calm scene. Suddenly, there was a scream. The silhouette of a young lady could be seen plunging into the water alongside the boat. Everyone gasped and yelled, but no one took action to help the young lady. Eventually, the people saw another figure plunging into the water alongside her. Life buoys were thrown to them and both were rescued. The passengers saw that the other person who'd gone into the water with the young lady was the old man! As the two wet people were brought up to the deck, other passengers viewed the old man in awe. They cried, "Speech! Speech! Tell us what motivated you!"

The old man looked carefully into the eyes of the people who surrounded him. Finally he said, "I have just one question—who pushed me?"

Who pushed me? That is what many Christians think when they spend time in the Scriptures. They feel as if they are obliged to do it; so, reluctantly, they do. It is not fun. It does not seem to have much of a positive impact on their lives.

The first objective of this chapter is to show you how beneficial it is for you to study and apply the Scriptures to your life. Look at some benefits mentioned in the Bible:

> The testimony of the Lord is sure, making wise the simple. The precepts of the Lord are right, rejoicing the heart; the commandment of the Lord is pure, enlightening the eyes (Psalm 19:7b, 8). Thy word is a lamp to my feet, and a light to my path (Psalm 119:105).

> Thy commandments make me wiser than my enemies, for they are ever mine. I have more light than all my teachers, for Thy testimonies are my meditation. I understand more than the aged, because I have observed Thy precepts (Psalm 119:98-100).

> If you abide in My word, then you are truly disciples of Mine; and you shall know the truth, and the truth shall make you free (John 8:31b,32).

As we study God's Word, we literally become more aware of what truth is. We become more enlightened. We become wiser than people who do not know and believe God's Word. We live better, happier, more fruitful lives. Our minds grow sharper and more useful to us. And Scripture gives a point of surety from which we can go forward; we don't have to debate over what is "truth."

We have definitely experienced this. The more we have studied the Scriptures, the better our minds have become at analysis in general. We have also become more sure of what is right and experience fewer doubts as to what action to take in a given situation. We find we have an increasing awareness of how unsure (and often very wrong) even learned people are when they do not possess the absolute truths of the Bible.

For example, some intelligent, well-meaning persons say that pornography does not hurt people and will not cause them to be more prone to the type of sexual behavior portrayed in the pornographic literature and films. It's not difficult to understand why they want to think that is true. After all, they reason, surely mature adults can control their behavior, can view these kinds of materials and keep them in perspective.

It sounds good — but it doesn't ring true to the teachings of the Word of God. In Proverbs 23:7 we have already read that we are what we think about. In Romans 12:2 Paul explains that we dare not conform ourselves to the ways of the world. Our very transformation into the kind of person God wants us to be depends crucially on the renewing of our minds. According to the Scriptures, our thought life leads eventually to our action life. Christians don't need to wonder about that; they can know it.

God's Word Affects Lives

Once you know what is right, you can focus your energies on implementation rather than further study and debate. One illustration of this comes to mind concerning Steve's relationship with his wife, Judy. Before they were married, Judy owned a little white dog named Loki. Steve inherited Loki when they married. Loki is basically a nice dog, but he does have a few undesirable characteristics. At times, Loki does not take care of matters well enough before they go to bed. As a result, sometimes he needs to be taken out in the middle of the night. He is housebroken and realizes he needs to be let out. You would think, since Judy owned him for many years before getting married, that he would awaken her. But she does not awaken easily in the middle of the night. So, instead, Loki scratches Steve on the arm to alert him to his need.

This occurred one cold and windy night. Steve had gone to bed late and was very sleepy. He cast a quick glance over at Judy. She was still asleep. The thought passed through his mind that it would be very appropriate for her to take Loki out, especially since it was her dog. Steve really didn't feel like taking Loki out. Then God brought to his mind the passage of Scripture that he'd been studying that day. It was 1 John 3:23: "And this is His commandment, that we believe in the name of His Son Jesus Christ, and love one

another, just as He commmanded us." Steve realized that God was
pointing to him that it was not a very loving thing for him to awaken
his wife. After all, he was already awake. She needed her sleep,
too. So, he took Loki out, returned to bed, and went back to sleep.
God used the passage Steve had been studying to improve his
behavior and his attitude toward his wife.

We Need to Get into the Word

Yes, God *can* enlighten us from His Word. We move now from
"why" to "how." The key question for you is, "Are you being enlightened from His Word?" Obviously that will not occur unless you get
into the Word. If that has not already been your practice, you may
ask, "How do I go about doing that?" Here are five suggestions:
1. Learn to like to study the Scriptures.
2. Pray for enlightenment.
3. Learn how to dig into the Scriptures.
4. Have a plan.
5. Spend the time.
Now, let's examine each point in detail.

1. LEARN TO LIKE TO STUDY THE SCRIPTURES.

On a daily basis it is very difficult to do something that we basically
do not like to do. As a result, our advice to you is to learn to like
to study the Word. That may sound difficult, yet God has caused
both of us to come to that point.

Here are some of the ways He can do that for you: One way is
to pray that God will give you the motivation to study His Word.
We know it is His will that we study His Word. So, if we ask in faith,
we can trust that He will make it a part of our lives.

As noted earlier, Philippians 2:13 reads, "For it is God who is at
work in you, both to will and to work for His good pleasure."

To paraphrase that, we could say, God is first willing to give us
the desire, and then to implement our doing it.

Earlier in this chapter, we mentioned some very great benefits
which come to you by studying God's Word. Meditate on those.
Begin to absorb the significance of these benefits to you personally.

Another specific benefit of studying God's Word is that it keeps
us from sin. Consider Psalm 119:11: "Thy word I have treasured in
my heart, that I may not sin against Thee."

Steve enjoys studying God's Word because it promises to improve him. He finds that it makes him live life at a level that he really would like to live and at which he knows God would like him to live. Studying God's Word also has the benefit of helping him know the Lord; for that is one of His primary ways of revealing Himself. Studying God's Word has the specific benefit of making us better people with whom to live. Perhaps that's more benefit to those around us than it is to us personally. Frankly, it's also a benefit to study God's Word because it's really fascinating to dig in and understand what it is saying.

As you study God's Word, you'll discover benefits that are meaningful to you. To remember them better, write them down on a sheet of paper. Keep that before you each time you study the Bible. This will help you enjoy reading it.

Another technique for learning to like studying the Bible is to read it with someone you like. About the time he made his commitment to Christ, Lee was so hungry to know God's will for his life that he got up anywhere from 2 to 5 o'clock in the morning to read the Bible. Then he began meeting with some mature Christians at 6:30 a.m. on Thursdays to study the Bible and pray. This, along with his desire and opportunity to learn to pray more effectively, soon gave Lee a clear, new direction in his life. Through this, God gave him guidance and success beyond what he had asked for or dreamed of receiving.

Lee believes, "People tend to do what they want, and make excuses for the rest." Therefore, if we are going to make a habit of spending time in the Scriptures, we need to learn to like it.

2. PRAY FOR ENLIGHTENMENT.

In 1 John 2:27 we read, "And as for you, the anointing which you received from Him abides in you, and you have no need for anyone to teach you; but as His anointing teaches you about all things, and is true and is not a lie, and just as it is taught you, you abide in Him."

What's being talked about here is the part of the Holy Spirit's role in our lives. He will help us study God's Word specifically, and give us wisdom that would otherwise escape us. So, don't forget to ask for His help.

See the previous chapter, "Praying for Wisdom," for more details on how to do this.

3. LEARN HOW TO DIG INTO THE SCRIPTURES.

One of the common problems that people have in understanding the Bible is that they really don't know how to study it. Many different techniques can be used in this. The following is a popular Bible-study technique that has been very helpful to Steve. It has been widely taught by Dr. Howard Hendricks, a professor and chairman of the department of Christian Education at Dallas Theological Seminary.

1. Observe. (What do you see?)
2. Interpret. (What does it mean?)
3. Apply. (What does it mean to you?)
4. Correlate. (Where does it fit?)

See the details on this in Chapter 9, "Reading," under the "Focus" point. This is a basic study help which can be used for digging into a whole passage, a verse, or even just a word or two. Every day Steve uses it to help him learn and apply in order to get the most from his time studying the Bible.

Whatever method you use, really get into the passage. Put yourself in the shoes (sandals) of the people mentioned. Feel with them, think with them. Picture the details. Live through the action.

When really digging into a passage, the results can be fascinating and sometimes even humorous. For example, one day Steve was studying Mark 6:45-52. The background of the passage is that Jesus had sent the twelve out to minister, heal and cast out demons. They came back all excited about things they wanted to tell Jesus. Unfortunately at that time in Capernaum there were lots of people around. The disciples couldn't really get into the deep, exciting and personal things. So, Jesus wisely suggested they row across the lake and find a lonely place to be together.

There was only one problem: The crowd saw where He was going, and they followed Him right around the lake. The sea of Galilee is not very large. You can see all the way across the lake, so it is no problem to track the progress of a boat on it. As a result, just about the time the disciples were docking the boat on the east side of the lake the crowd pressed in. Jesus felt compassion on the people because of their needs. At the end of that day He performed a miraculous feeding of the entire crowd.

There is every reason to believe that the disciples were a little bit irritated. They wanted to have a retreat with Jesus and it hadn't happened. He had been talking to the crowd.

Now we come to the events of this passage. In that context consider verse 45: "And immediately He made His disciples get into the boat and go ahead of Him to the other side to Bethsaida, while He Himself was sending the multitude away."

This is at the end of the day. You would surely think Jesus would want to keep the disciples around to help dismiss the crowd, wouldn't you? Unless, of course, they weren't any help. And that was the case. So, He made them leave.

Then He dismissed the crowd and departed to the nearby mountain to pray. From this point He could easily be in line of sight with the disciples' boat.

Now we pick up with verses 47 and 48: "And when it was evening, the boat was in the midst of the sea, and He was alone on the land. And seeing them straining at the oars, for the wind was against them, at about the fourth watch of the night, He came to them . . . ." You may happen to have in the margin of your Bible a note stating that this watch was from 3-6 a.m. Do you realize how long those disciples had been out rowing in the middle of the lake? They were there from about six or seven the previous evening until about 4 o'clock in the morning. Yet, it's only about two to four miles across the lake at this point. How upset those disciples must have been! They were rowing against a heavy wind. When they could have just drifted over to the shore and waited for better weather. Probably they were so angry that they weren't willing to be reasonable.

What is interesting is that Jesus let them stay out there for a long time. He could see them (v. 48), but He let them stew for awhile. There is an application here. How long are we willing to stay angry, "rowing against a head wind"? Sometimes God lets us stew for awhile until we admit our problem.

Well, here comes the really funny part (v. 48), "He came to them, walking on the sea; and He intended to pass by them." Can you imagine what had to have been going through Jesus' mind? He had to be a little amused. Surely He knew what the disciples were going to think when they saw Him walking on the water. What's more, He wasn't even planning to stop. "Come along, boys. I'll be waiting for you at the shore." Apparently, He was willing to let them stay in their state until they cried for help.

Well, gratefully, they did cry for help in the next verse, "But when they saw Him walking on the sea, they supposed that it was a ghost, and cried out [That's understandable!], for they all saw Him and were frightened. But immediately He spoke with them and said to them, 'Take courage; it is I, do not be afraid.' And He got into the boat with them, and the winds stopped; and they were greatly astonished, for they had not gained any insight from the incident of the loaves, but their heart was hardened."

As we see how Jesus had to deal with his disciples when they

were not in a spiritual state, we gain insight into how He may have to deal with us, too. It gives us incentive to confess our sins quickly.

As we dig into the detail of what's going on in the Word, it becomes extremely fascinating. Sometimes what goes on is funny. In these passages we see the geography, we sense the timing, we feel the interpersonal moods. We then can make the best application to our lives.

4. HAVE A PLAN.

Almost every activity in life benefits from some planning. Learning from the Scriptures is no exception. If we are serious about it and really want to be sure we do it, we need to plan for it.

As you will find out further in the chapter on planning, every good plan has objectives. These are specific targets which we seek to achieve. With regard to our use of the Word of God, there are five objectives. These objectives are detailed below, along with some suggested ways to implement them. Each of them in some way helps us obtain and apply wisdom from the Scriptures.

Worshiping and Communicating with God

One of the most powerful ways to use the Word of God is to let it help enhance our relationship with God. The Bible is our most elaborate description of God — His character and His actions toward men. As we see Him as He really is, we are forced to our knees in worship and adoration of Him. We find ourselves saying with David,

> "I will extol Thee, my God, O King; and I will bless Thy name forever and ever. Every day I will bless Thee, and I will praise Thy name forever and ever. Great is the Lord, and highly to be praised; and His greatness is unsearchable" (Psalm 145:1-3).

As this illustrates, we often will find ourselves communicating with God in the words of the Scriptures. In our prayers we also will claim scriptural promises, mention scriptural principles and in other ways base our communication with God on His Word.

To accomplish this objective you need to spend regular time reading the Scriptures. You should have at least one such time daily. As you are reading and studying, pause occasionally and "relate" to God. Talk to Him; worship Him; praise Him. Let the topic of your conversation flow from what you have been reading.

Pointing Out Needs in Our Lives

As we read the Scriptures, God convicts us of areas where He wants us to improve and grow. This is a very important part of the wisdom we can obtain from the Scriptures.

In our personal Bible study, we need to be sure to read a wide spectrum of Scripture over a period of time. One good way to do this is to read through the entire Bible every year or so. We should make sure we don't specialize our study on only certain topics or passages. That limits the raw material with which the Spirit can work as He seeks to point out weaknesses in our lives.

Meeting Needs in Our Lives

The Scriptures are the best source of information on how to meet needs in our lives. If we have questions, the first place to look for authoritative answers is the Bible. If we wonder how others have confronted these types of problems, there may be examples of people with similar problems in the Bible. If we need to be comforted, we can turn to appropriate passages in the Bible and have that need met.

To do this, you usually have to do some form of topical study. You normally start with a word or topic and then check a reference as to what the Bible has to say on that subject. A concordance (such as Cruden's, Strong's or Young's, with the latter two tied to original Greek or Hebrew words) is designed to help you find Bible verses which contain a given word. A topical Bible (such as Nave's) quotes whole verses and passages on a given topic. Bible dictionaries and encyclopedias can help your study on some subjects.

Bible handbooks and commentaries can help in your analysis of given passages. Some Bible editions, such as the Scofield Reference Bible, the Thompson New Chain-Reference Bible and the Open Bible, have concordances, cyclopedic indices, cross references and other reference aids built right into them. In addition, there are many books available to give various other kinds of help in your personal Bible study (see details in the further study material section at the end of this book).

If you want to know more about these and other reference materials, a visit to your church's or pastor's library or to a good Christian bookstore would probably be very helpful. There you can actually see samples and ask how to use them.

Sometimes you will have time to do a thorough study in an area of long-term need. At other times you will simply go to the Scriptures and quickly find a passage that meets the need of the moment.

For example, the December after Judy and Steve got married, Steve was in the Philippines for two weeks. His plan was to go straight from there to his home town of Rockford, Illinois. Judy was to meet him there the weekend before Christmas. His mother had planned a wedding reception for them at the Douglass's home church.

Steve's flight schedule called for him to go from Manila to Tokyo and then to Chicago. Judy was flying to Chicago at about the same time. Steve's sister and her husband were planning to pick them both up and drive them to Rockford.

The plane took off from Manila about an hour late—but this was nothing to be alarmed about. Sometime during the flight, the steward came by and handed Steve a card to fill out to enter Japan. He explained that he wouldn't need that since he would be staying in the transit lounge until his Chicago flight departed.

He looked at Steve with a puzzled face, "Haven't you heard?"
"Heard what?"
"That the Northwest flight to Chicago has been cancelled."

At once, Steve's mind was flooded with many thoughts and feelings. *It can't be true! This is unfair! I am going to miss my own wedding reception. My mother has been planning this for months. She is going to be so disappointed. What can I do?*

After a few minutes of severe disappointment, Steve pulled out his Bible and began leafing through the Psalms and praying intermittently. Slowly, his heart calmed as he referenced various verses on peace and trust in God. There were several of these in the first several Psalms, especially 3:3-5. Eventually he became joyful and thanked God for this opportunity to trust Him. Then, as the psalmist said in 3:5, ("He lay down and slept,") Steve literally took a nap.

When he arrived in Tokyo, the airlines tried to get him to stay overnight there and fly out with them the next day. Instead, after much negotiation, they transferred him to another airline. He started working his way toward the Chicago airport. There was no assurance that he would get there in time. He had no reservations from Los Angeles (where he was landing) to Chicago; it was the weekend before Christmas and one airline was on strike. All other airlines were overbooked.

Occasionally during the various flights Steve would return to the Psalms for comfort as the need arose. He arrived at the Chicago airport at 4 o'clock in the morning—in time to make it to his own wedding reception. God was gracious to work things out. But He was also gracious to meet Steve's need for peace through His Word.

Displacing Less Fruitful Thoughts

When we are thinking about God and His Word we can't easily

be entertaining thoughts of sin or unfruitful activities. Consider the following: "Thy word have I treasured in my heart, that I may not sin against Thee" (Psalm 119:11).

"Finally brethren, whatever is true, whatever is honorable, whatever is right, whatever is pure, whatever is lovely, whatever is of good repute, if there is any excellence and if anything worthy of praise, let your mind dwell on these things" (Philippians 4:8).

As we fill our hearts and minds with the Word of God, it is not hard to understand how we can lead lives that are positive, godly and wise.

You may ask, "How can you focus on the Scriptures in a way that displaces other thoughts?" One practical way is to listen to tapes of the Scriptures and music based on the Scriptures. Soon, you will find yourself quoting or singing along.

Another excellent way is to memorize Scripture on a regular basis. Scripture memory cards and programs are available. See Chapter 13 for help in memorizing.

A third way is to meditate on Scripture. This can easily be coupled with the other two approaches. As you listen to or call to mind a Scripture, mull it over in your mind. Think of its meaning and its application to you. Say it over in your mind. Picture the action or image of the verse. If you have trouble remembering it, write it on a card and place the card where you will see it often during the day.

Telling Others About God

Paul said to his disciple Timothy, "And these things which you have heard from me in the presence of many witnesses, these entrust to faithful men, who will be able to teach others also" (2 Timothy 2:2). One of the most satisfying results of Bible study is the opportunity to help others with what we have found and learned.

In order to do this, we must normally first apply the truth to our own lives. As it takes on the reality of being lived through us, we become more relevant to others.

Sometimes we can help our own Bible study and application by teaching others. For example, every week Steve has to have something fresh from the Word of God which is relevant and helpful to the members of his Sunday school class. That encourages him to keep studying, even if he doesn't feel exceptionally motivated some mornings.

Another stimulus to obtaining wisdom from the Scriptures is taking opportunities to share the message of Christ with those who don't know Him. The questions of a person who sincerely wants to know more about God provide motive enough to send almost any of us to the Bible to learn more.

5. SPEND THE TIME.

The fifth suggestion on how to obtain wisdom from the Scriptures: Spend the time. Every one of the actions mentioned above takes some time. Listening to a tape of Scriptures in the car may only involve turning on the tape player, but many of the other actions require time to be set aside regularly and it should be every day. In this time you can read, pray, worship, discern needs, meet needs, meditate, memorize, apply and prepare. Pick a time when you are normally alert and motivated and which can influence you for the day. David apparently spent special time with God every morning, for he wrote, "In the morning, O Lord, Thou wilt hear my voice; in the morning I will order my prayer to Thee and eagerly watch" (Psalm 5:3).

Whatever time of the day you pick, be sure to set aside enough time. The exact amount will depend on your walk with God and on your needs. For someone who isn't at all used to a regular Bible study time, five minutes per day may be a major accomplishment. For anyone desiring to mature rapidly in his faith, five minutes will certainly be inadequate. Some people suggest a minimum of thirty minutes, others suggest an hour. Pick an amount of time that is somewhat stretching, but definitely possible for you. Remember a fabulous amount of practical wisdom for living life is available to you in the Scriptures. Can you afford not to spend an adequate length of time?

However much time you set aside, be sure to honor it. One of the greatest barriers to a special time of Bible study and prayer is not getting around to it. There seem to be two kinds of people in the morning: leapers and creepers. If you are a creeper, you may want to have your time just before you go to bed in the evening.

Regardless of your natural alertness in the morning, you will normally find it hard to squeeze that time in before your other commitments of the day begin. Set your alarm a little earlier. "Oh," you say, "but then I won't get enough sleep."

Now we are getting to the real problem: when do you go to bed? It's hard to soar with both the owls and the eagles. What keeps you up so late? For many people, it is television. If that is the case with you, the real secret to a successful Bible study and prayer time will be to discipline yourself to turn off the set and go to bed.

And when you set your alarm, move it far enough away so that you really have to wake up to shut if off. When it goes off, find some way to leave the bed – roll off, if necessary. Then splash water on your face; go to another room; turn on some bright lights – do whatever you must to become fully awake. Steve says he thinks better standing up – especially in the morning. So, he often studies the Bible standing up and sometimes walking around.

As a last bit of motivation on this point, Steve tells of something that happened to him one Saturday a few years ago. He intended to have his special time with God, but kept putting it off. He had to run for exercise, wash the car, take a bath, eat breakfast, and read the newspaper. Among other things, that day he had to buy a refrigerator and deliver it. Some friends had already rented a trailer and Steve had to rush over to their house to borrow it while it was available – still not getting around to his Bible study and prayer time. He kept saying, "I'll do that just after I get through with this next item." Instead, though, he kept doing other things.

When he went to the first appliance store, he was sure they had what he wanted at the right price. But they didn't. He went to the second place. No refrigerator. God kept saying, "Are you going to spend time with Me?" Steve's response seemed to be, "I'll get to it; don't worry."

Finally, as if he was providing a compromise for God, he went to the Salvation Army store – that seemed like a spiritual source of refrigerators. Sure enough, there was his refrigerator – just the right price and just the right size. He bought it. By now the store was closing. They were in a hurry to lock the gates, so he didn't really tie the refrigerator onto the trailer very well.

He headed onto a particularly bumpy stretch of freeway. The refrigerator started to rock back and forth. The cord snapped, the refrigerator spun around and slammed against the back of the trailer and it started to tip over onto the highway.

Traffic was scattering everywhere to get out of the way. Steve noticed all this just in time. He slammed on the brakes and the refrigerator miraculously tipped back upright, still in the trailer.

That was good, but that wasn't the end. God wasn't through with Steve yet. This refrigerator had the freezer on the bottom, so the freezer door slammed against the trailer railing and stayed shut. Unfortunately, however, the impact caused the main refrigerator door to pop open. The bottom shelf shot the two crisper drawers into the traffic behind him. As he pulled over to the side of the highway, he witnessed several cars playing hockey with one of the crisper-drawer "pucks." Finally a Pinto scored a goal on Steve's side of the highway. He retrieved his battered crisper drawers and went home.

Looking back on that day, Steve now says, "I am sad to think of what God had to do to get my attention that day — all because I wouldn't spend time in His Word."

SUMMARY

In summary, we receive many benefits when we study the Scriptures. One of them is that they offer tremendous wisdom for our minds to use in making sound judgments. In order to receive these benefits we need to:
1. Learn to like to study the Scriptures.
2. Pray for enlightenment.
3. Learn how to dig into the Scriptures.
4. Have a plan.
5. Spend the time.

Before leaving this chapter, be sure to make an entry in the Personal Application Worksheet as indicated below.

— — —

I. PERSONAL APPLICATION

What is your highest personal priority application point found in the principles in this chapter? (For example, you might feel "setting aside the time for Bible study" is your most pressing need at this time.) Enter your top application point in the indicated place on the Personal Application Worksheet at the end of the book. Next, enter in the column to the right some specific plans to help you start implementing your application point. Although by now you should be proficient with this, we've included a couple of sample implementation steps relating to our sample priority application point above:

1. Set aside 30 minutes or more every morning starting at 6:00 to study the Word of God.
2. Shut off the television earlier and make a point of getting to bed by 10:30.
3. Ask my wife to study for a portion of that time with me. This will help motivate me to actually follow through.

II. THOUGHT QUESTIONS

1. What are some of the benefits mentioned in the Bible of studying God's Word?
2. What are some practical barriers which interfere with my study of the Bible? How can I get around these barriers?
3. What specific passage, story or topic in Scripture would I most like to dig into now and why?
4. Which of the five objectives of Scriptures mentioned in this chapter am I applying in my life? How can I start applying the Scriptures in some new ways?

III. ACTION PROJECT

List the top five areas where you need wisdom over the next several weeks. Select from those the highest priority area about which you think the Scriptures would have the most to say. Design a plan for the next week to dig into the Scriptures specifically to find some answers to your questions. How are you going to locate the best passages to study? How are you going to tackle the passages to get your answers? Do any of the personalities or circumstances portrayed in the Bible shed any light on your questions?

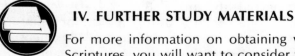

IV. FURTHER STUDY MATERIALS

For more information on obtaining wisdom from the Scriptures, you will want to consider the Further Study Materials for this chapter listed at the end of the book

6

OBSERVING

Two drivers came upon the scene of a one-car accident just after it had happened. After determining that the car's sole occupant had not been hurt, the other motorists began to survey the damaged car. One man saw liquid dripping onto the ground about a foot behind one of the rear tires. Somewhat panicked, he yelled, "It looks like gas leaking from the tank!"

The other man bent near the dripping liquid, wet his finger with it, smelled it, and said, "Nothing to worry about. It's just water." They opened the trunk and discovered a plastic water jug had broken during the accident.

What the first man learned from that incident was to observe more carefully before jumping to a conclusion. That is a lesson most people need to apply.

Let's suppose you walk by a friend at work and he doesn't smile at you. You might conclude that he has something against you and then start to worry about it. When you finally get around to asking your friend about it, he says he simply was lost in thought and didn't even notice you had passed by. His face had given evidence that he was deep in thought, but all you had noticed was that he hadn't smiled.

How many of our problems would be solved if we were just more observant? How many of our relationships with others would be enhanced if we would listen more carefully? How much better would our thinking be if we could sense things more clearly?

For most of us the answer is, "A lot!"

Jesus said, "The lamp of the body is the eye; if therefore your eye is clear, your whole body will be full of light. But if your eye is bad, your whole body will be full of darkness" (Matthew 6:22,23a). Among other things, Jesus is establishing the principle that our senses are the gateways of information to us. If our senses are faulty (or if we use them in a faulty manner), we suffer as a result. We can only think and act upon that which we have observed.

During a typical day we observe many different kinds of things such as scenery, physical objects around the house, people, television, written words, and pictures. As we observe these things there are two main characteristics we look for: physical characteristics (color, size, weight, shape) and symbolic characteristics (words, numbers, signs, letters). Normally, when we look at a tree we are looking at its physical characteristics such as size, color and texture. Normally, when we read words on a page of a book we are looking at the symbolic characteristics such as words, sentence structure and context.

In this chapter we will present a basic approach that contains principles which can be used for either kind of observation. To explain the technique to you, we will use physical characteristic examples. We believe this will be the best way for you to understand the principles initially. The next chapter will go on from observing to interpreting and organizing. The two following chapters will present how to apply observing, interpreting and organizing methods to the two most common symbolic observation situations: listening and reading.

With this overview as a background, let's begin to learn how to observe.

Preliminary Steps

As with every conscious activity of our minds, we should begin our observing by *praying* and *concentrating*.

First, take a moment to ask God for wisdom as we have spoken of before. Jesus said, "And I will ask the Father, and He will give you another Helper, that He may be with you forever; that is the Spirit of truth . . . but the Helper, the Holy Spirit, whom the Father will send in My name, He will teach you all things. . . ." (John 14:16-17,26).

Second, concentrate on observing. A moment of focused mental effort may contribute more to your conscious awareness than weeks or even years of casual observation. For example, think of some stairway you often climb. How many steps are there? Most people would answer, "I don't know." Why? Is it because they haven't had enough exposure to that fact to know? No; they well may have climbed the stairs every day for years. They simply have never bothered to count them.

We constantly are exposed to many objects that we could observe, so we have learned to "tune some of them out." This is not all bad, as we will discuss later. But in order to do a first class job of observing, we have to break out of that frame of mind and consciously focus our minds on what we should be noticing.

The Process of Observing

The essence of observing is describing. You determine concepts and words, specifically, which describe a physical object or situation. From the many alternative colors, you determine it to be red, or whatever. From many alternative shapes, you determine it to be square. From various possible tastes, you determine it to be sweet. You describe, describe, and continue to describe. That is what observation is.

The process of observing or describing has four steps which make the acrostic SAFE:

1. Scan.
2. Ask.
3. Focus.
4. Explore.

Now let's consider each step in detail.

1. SCAN.

The purpose of this step is first to be sure we have the "big picture." This does two important things for us. First, it gives us the widest possible selection from which we can choose certain specifics for more careful scrutiny. Second, it provides a context for proper observation and interpretation.

Lest you think this is a theoretical point, let us tell you a little incident which occurred a few years ago. A man and his wife had driven their car to Colorado State University where they were attending a Campus Crusade for Christ staff training conference. Although it was summer, the weather turned very cold one day and the clouds were darker than usual. It started to rain and eventually began to hail. When the husband saw the hail, he ran out to the car to drive it under a big tree. He made it to the tree, but unfortunately the hailstorm then became unbelievably bad. Many of the hailstones were as big as golf balls and some as big as baseballs. (Honest! This is no fish story.)

The tree was only somewhat helpful and at the end of the storm, the car had many dents in it. When the owner drove his car back to where it had originally been parked, he made an interesting observation. He was only a hundred feet from a wide pedestrian walkway under a nearby building. It would have provided perfect protection for his car, but he had not even noticed it. In his observation process he had never scanned the scene.

As you are scanning, "verbalize" in your mind what you are seeing. This forces you to make more than a "once-over-lightly" kind of look. You might try this technique: Compare what you are seeing to other objects of a similar kind. For example, if you see a tree, is it "big" or "small" or "in between," in relation to trees you have seen previously? You may even know the type of tree it is. If so, name it in your mind.

Move along from item to item fairly quickly, taking no more than a few seconds on any one item for this step. Sometimes you may find it helpful to react a little to cause your mind to participate enough to observe.

Look for specific objects or characteristics, and for relationships between them.

Be sure to absorb information from all of your senses. You might otherwise use only your sight in the scanning step. Run down a checklist in your mind:

> What do I see?
> What do I hear?
> What do I smell?
> What do I feel?
> What do I taste?

A certain executive runs for exercise in the mornings. When he is away from home on a trip, there is an added mental dimension which could probably best be described as scanning. As he runs, he notes street names and landmarks so he will be able to find his way back. He also notices gas stations, when they are open, and what they charge for gas. He notices hotels and motels and public facilities such as convention centers, sports arenas and parks. He looks for restaurants and what they specialize in serving. He looks for grocery stores, banks, shops. By the time he returns from his run, he has surveyed the neighborhood. If he needs to buy gas or eat at a restaurant or cash a check, he will know where to go. He is giving himself more alternatives from which to choose in the future. In addition, this helps keep his mind alert and processing.

2. ASK.

From the many details you could observe in depth, ask which few seem relevant to you at that time. For example, when you are driving a car, you *must* observe activities of other cars on the road in front, as well as traffic signals and the road's course. If you don't observe these carefully enough, you may have an accident. For most people, the appearance of houses and lawns along the roadway are items of casual but not focused observation. On the other hand, if you are an architect, horticulturalist, or a real estate agent, you may desire to focus on houses and lawns as you travel in a car.

What you select to scrutinize is normally determined by your needs, your interests, and your perspective. Most needs that demand our attention are along the lines of what to eat or what to wear. If you want to observe people who are scanning, asking, and focusing on action watch people who are going through a buffet line at a restaurant or shopping at a department store sale.

The main point we are making here is that it is normal to "ask" if it is worth observing some things more closely. Some people tend to gloss over virtually everything and never become meaningfully observant of anything. They are starving their minds. Without the raw material of observations, the mind cannot turn out much product in the way of thought and insight. The key starting point of good Bible study, for example, is "observation." We can benefit only from what we notice.

But some people select too soon. They don't take enough time to look around at the alternatives. They prematurely jump to conclusions. The penalty they pay is that they often don't take full advantage of the circumstances they face.

For example, one man we know could have paid that penalty one time when he was invited to make use of a carpenter's shop. No one else was going to be there. The man had the key and all the materials he needed. When he arrived at the shop, he could not find the main light switch. He searched and searched and could only succeed in getting the entrance way light on. In his observing, though, he didn't limit himself to the traditional places for light switches. He looked in the cabinets as well. In the process, he found a portable hanging light which met his need. Instead of having to go home disappointed, he was able to rig up enough light to do the work he came to do.

Another warning in this area is, "Don't get in a rut!" Our natural interests and perspectives tend to lead us to select similar types of things to observe. To have a specialty is good; to be handicapped by it is bad. At least occasionally, force yourself outside of your normal routine of observation into a new area. Listen carefully to the music of a song; watch a sports activity that is different from your main interest; try to identify all the different "smells" in a room (coming from the walls, furniture, books, or rug). Generally, our creativity level is raised when it is stimulated by new observations.

You have probably never plumbed the depths of all observations that could be made about a given room or situation or object. Perhaps you have heard the story of the two old women rocking on their front porch. In the distance an orchestra was playing in an outdoor amphitheater. In the women's yard, crickets were chirping. One lady was listening to the music and said, "Isn't that beautiful?" The other was listening to the crickets and said, "Yes it is. And I understand they make the sound by rubbing their legs together."

3. FOCUS.

Once you have scanned the situation and asked about which things are worthy of your further attention, you then can focus on them. Really concentrate. Dig in. Stretch your mind and use your observing skills. Bring the key facts to the surface and consciously note them. Doing this involves developing a certain amount of discipline, and it involves sharpening your senses.

To assist you in developing in these areas we would like to give you a few assignments. We think you will find them very enlightening.

ASSIGNMENT #1:

Sit in the driver's seat of your automobile and see how many "control devices" on the vehicle are within your reach. Include the door handles, windshield wiper switch, ignition switch, and steering wheel. You'll be amazed to discover probably more than 50 such control devices.

ASSIGNMENT #2:

Carefully observe as many things as you can about your dwelling place from the following positions:
1. From a distance (100-200 feet away)
2. From just outside the front door
3. From just inside the front door
4. From one of the chairs where a guest would likely sit when visiting you.

During such observation, several unsightly items may come to your attention which you can remove or fix.

The perspectives above are those a person has when he visits you at home. These are the raw materials from which that person might form a first impression about you. You can see, then, how important it is for you to observe these things carefully from time to time, lest you inadvertently send an undesirable message to someone about yourself.

ASSIGNMENT #3:

Think of some common object in your home. Set it before you. See how many descriptive words you can use concerning the object. If you are at a loss for something to use, try a lump of ground beef. See how quickly you can note 20 observable facts about ground beef.

Review your experience in these assignments. You spent more time focusing on each item than normal. You were more thoughtful and thorough. You probably passed your eyes across the dashboard of your car very systematically. You may have written down your list of observations and been stimulated by the types of items on the list to think of other similar items. You have specifically gone through the checklist mentioned earlier in the chapter.

You may have experienced more general sensations. You may have liked or disliked what you observed. We will cover that more in the context of interpretation, but no observation should be set aside. Many times our intuitive sense is very accurate.

You consciously noticed details you may have been overlooking for a long time. That is what focusing is all about.

Some people think that the main key to being a good artist is to have good hands. While steady hands are naturally important to an artist, the crucial skill is having the ability to observe. This has been dramatically proven in recent years by Joni Eareckson Tada. This young woman is totally paralyzed from the neck down, yet today she is widely known for her artistic ability. She cannot use her hands, but her artwork is so good that someone not knowing her handicap would have no way of knowing that she draws entirely by holding a pen or brush in her mouth.

A person's observation abilities can be improved through practice and discipline. Newspaper reporters, police detectives, professional writers, and job placement directors are superb observation analysts. Their daily work makes them focus, scrutinize, question, research and analyze everything around them. In time, their keen powers of observation become part of their natural make-up. With practice, you, too, could develop such powers of observation.

4. EXPLORE.

Your observing will often be incomplete if you do not conduct certain "explorations" or "experiments." Focusing is a mental process whereas exploring is mostly a physical act of experimentation which adds to our observations.

For example, suppose we see a three-inch by five-inch, ivory-colored plaque on the wall by the door, with a one-half-inch plastic armature sticking out of the center of it. That's interesting, but it probably isn't going to do much for us until we put that together in our mind with some past experience and conclude that it is a light switch. Now, that opens up the possibility of some additional observation. Which light does it control? We can very easily explore or experiment to find that out by reaching over to the switch and flipping it to the "on" position. Then we can look around the room and observe which lights went on. Apart from thinking about our initial observation and responding, we would not have truly observed all of the characteristics of that light switch.

As you are observing, ask if there is something you should move in order to see beyond it. Perhaps you simply need to change your position by a few feet. Should you touch or push an object to learn more of its texture and weight and steadiness? Should you make a sound to see if the object is alive? Should you mix it with water to see if it dissolves? Should you heat it up to see if it changes? Should you try it out to see how it works?

All of these are further explorations beyond passive observation. You now become an active participant.

Many times the additional effort is not worth it in light of your purposes. But do think of exploring each time you observe and realize that some facts cannot be observed without exploring.

SUMMARY

In summary, observing is describing. It is done best when we pray and concentrate on it. The process of observing is done in four steps:

1. Scan.
2. Ask.
3. Focus.
4. Explore.

To remember this approach, simply think of the first letter of each word: SAFE. This approach is a "safe" way to be sure you are observing carefully.

We *scan* to gain the big picture and to insure we are not ignoring some items. We *ask* the Lord and ourselves which items to observe more closely at a given time. We *focus* our senses and our minds on these items, seeking to be more thorough and systematic in our examination of them. We *explore*, when necessary, in order to observe more completely.

Most often the above process is sequential. As we encounter a situation, we scan, then select, and so on. Sometimes, however, we back-track in light of what we learn. For example, we may start to focus on something and discover it doesn't really warrant our focus or that it doesn't interest us. We may want to scan and select again.

Sometimes we simply don't want to work that hard at observing. When we are relaxing in the evening after a hard day, we may just want to turn on some soothing music, sink into a comfortable chair and not think about anything. Our observing then is more of a feeling or mood or general sensation, and we have no plans to act on anything (unless sleep can be considered an action).

What we observe becomes the raw material from which we fashion thoughts and decide to stimulate actions. Our observations are also stored in our minds for future reference. How important it is, therefore, for us to learn to observe well, if we want to make the most of our minds.

— — —

I. PERSONAL APPLICATION

What is your highest personal priority application point found in the principles presented in this chapter. Enter that point in the indicated place in the Personal Application Worksheet at the end of the book. In the column next to that enter some specific plans to help you start implementing that point.

II. THOUGHT QUESTIONS

1. Without looking back in this chapter, can I list the two preliminary points regarding how to observe?
2. Without looking back in the chapter, can I list the four steps in the process of observing as based on the acrostic SAFE?
3. What is the essence of observing?

4. Why is it important to go from pure mental observation to exploring?

III. ACTION PROJECT

Our guess is that you may not have completed the three action assignments given in the "Focus" point of this chapter. If not, take the time to try at least one of them. For example, the next time you hop into a car, see how many different control devices you have within your reach.

IV. FURTHER STUDY MATERIALS

For more information on observing, you will want to consider the Further Study Materials for this chapter listed at the end of the book.

7

INTERPRETING AND ORGANIZING

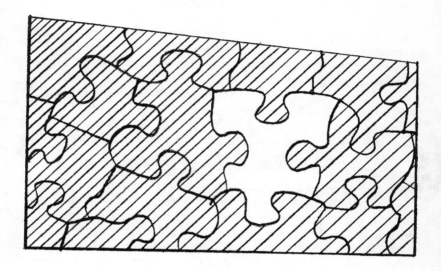

The Canadian ministry of Campus Crusade for Christ sponsors a college level basketball team. In addition to playing colleges, the team plays amateur club teams and national teams from various countries. A few years ago the team was scheduled to play the Soviet Union's team, which is one of the best amateur teams in the world. Rle Nichols, the coach of the Canadian team, did some extra homework in preparation for the game. He was looking for a weakness in the otherwise overwhelmingly strong team.

As he pored over films of previous Soviet games and gathered and analyzed other information, he discovered that the Soviet team was made up of predominantly right-handed players who could not dribble well to their left. They tended to dribble and move to their right.

The coach instructed the Canadian team players to defend the Soviet players by overshifting toward their right side. This forced the Soviet players toward the left and pushed them out of their natural play. The result was that the Canadian team won the game — because their coach was able to look at the facts, discern a key pattern, and act accordingly. This is an illustration of interpreting and organizing information.

Processing information in the mind involves activities such as: interpreting, organizing, generating ideas, solving problems, making decisions, planning, remembering and forgetting. The next two chapters are on listening and reading which, along with praying, studying the Scriptures and observing, are ways of entering information into the mind. After these there will be chapters on the other "processing" activities.

In this chapter we are going to talk about interpreting and organizing thoughts in our minds.

Interpreting is basically *explaining*. It involves determining the meaning of what is observed. It is the first step of comprehending the significance of what is observed.

Organizing is basically *relating*. It involves seeing connections, patterns, purposes and implications. It goes beyond interpretation to conceptualization and advanced comprehension. It is a core mental skill, called upon constantly to aid in interpreting, planning, decision-making and speaking.

Without the ability to interpret and organize information in our minds, we would be reduced to simple input/output devices in which every stimulus had some sort of predictable response. Our behavior could basically be described by a set of equations such as, "for every action there is an equal and opposite reaction." We all know that human beings are not that way. They are very complicated and sophisticated in their responses to situations. They often endure patiently under repeated, apparently severe hardships only to buckle under a seemingly minor circumstantial pressure. Part of the explanation of this relates to the context in which they interpret and respond to various situations.

It has been said that all men are rational in their own eyes. People feel their point of view on any given subject is justified. Then how can you explain people having different points of view on the same issue? Sometimes they don't possess the same facts. Sometimes, however, their differing views stem more from the way they interpret and organize the same set of "facts" differently in their minds. Quite a number of basketball teams played the Soviet team before Rle Nichol's team did. But few, if any, coaches were able to interpret the Soviet team's tendencies as strategically as Rle.

Two Important First Steps

Now let's consider how to interpret and organize our thoughts. *Prayer* and *concentration* are once again the basic first steps.

Just as Steve was in the middle of working on this chapter he received a phone call. The caller asked him to speak in place of a person who was ill. His schedule for the book was such that if he was going to make the progress necessary, his time had to be fairly uninterrupted. In fact, he had just been struggling with a major issue of how to organize some of the content of this chapter. All the pieces were in front of him, but the pattern was not clear. As Steve prayed and thought about whether to speak, he sensed God was telling him to go ahead and that He would more than make up that time lost on the book. He said yes and went back up to his desk to spend a half hour more on the book before going. As he started, he specifically prayed and asked God for a breakthrough in his thinking. Almost immediately his thoughts started flowing in a direction he had not considered before. Within that half hour the breakthrough idea was detailed on the paper in front of him.

The main point of telling this is to show how God supernaturally interacts with our minds in the area of interpreting and organizing our thoughts. The experience also reiterated to Steve how faithful God is to give back more than we ever give up in time and productivity. Through the power of God much can be accomplished in a concentrated period of time.

Be sure to make prayer and concentration an integral part of your observing, interpreting, organizing, and (as you will learn in the next two chapters) listening, reading, and studying. They are crucial. God can give insight in a moment that cannot be achieved by years of study.

The Processes of Interpreting and Organizing

In the last chapter you saw the outline:
1. Scan.
2. Ask.
3. Focus.
4. Explore.

It was applied to how to observe. The process of interpreting and organizing follows the same outline. The details of each step are different, but the basic concept is the same.

1. SCAN.

The way to start the process of interpreting and organizing in your mind is to scan all the facts that seem pertinent to what you are considering. Get the big picture. Look for the obvious meaning and pattern and purpose. Quickly ask yourself the six basic questions:

Who?
What?
When?
Where?
Why?
How?

Your observing may even be going on at the same time you are asking these questions; but as you seek to interpret, you will push further. "What" needs to be pushed beyond physical description to determining an apparent objective. "How" needs to be pushed beyond physical description to determining apparent functions. The details of what to look for in response to each of these questions, as it relates to interpreting and organizing, will be developed under the "focus" point below. But you should first look for the things that are easy to see.

If this sounds too complicated, let's look at a common illustration of this process in your daily life. As you proceed down a buffet line in a restaurant, you encounter facts which you observe. There are many variations in color, shape, texture, smell, and taste. Almost without any conscious mental effort, you quickly identify the items as certain foods which you are familiar with.

The analyzing going on in your mind is sophisticated and involved, but the patterns are so familiar to you the processing of the information is easy. Usually your eyes first observe certain physical characteristics of one entree. You check for color, shape, texture, number and size. The central processing area of your brain then sends a message to your memory to recall anything in the "food" category of these particular specifications. If it only sends one name, you have a match and know you are looking at a piece of chicken. If your memory sends down two or three alternatives, you have to decide which is the one on the basis of some more evidence. You may read the sign over the food; you may ask the person behind the counter; you may lean over and look more closely at the item. One way or another, you will probably receive sufficient information to satisfy your curiosity and move you to the next mental step, which is to determine if you want to eat that particular entree at this meal.

We take you through that explanation simply to point out that your mind is working hard almost all the time. It is usually on some form of "automatic pilot" as you subconsciously evaluate things. This is the dominant mode of operations in the scanning step. Sometimes you will run into a need for conscious thought, as when you didn't recognize the entree. At the scanning stage, though, you are moving right along, recognizing fairly quickly and without a great deal of effort the meanings and patterns and purposes of what you encounter.

Although much of this step occurs automatically, in order to do it well you might need to acquire a few new habits. You need to maintain a large base of items which you can quickly recognize. This sounds easy, but things change and you forget; so, you have to keep introducing your mind to new material. Curiosity is your best friend here. Cultivate it and try to satisfy it every chance you can. Read the labels on some new items on the shelf in the store, rather than just grabbing the same old items you buy every week. When you don't know, ask questions. Be attentive to the answers and you will be making a friend while you are learning something new. Specifically try to explain things you encounter, both to yourself and to someone else. If you have a young child handy, you will make a big hit answering all of his or her questions.

Try not to limit your exposure to the boundaries of your current habits and assumptions. From time to time go to a different store to jar yourself out of your routine and open your mind to new stimuli. Deliberately try some activity which is new to you, keeping an observant eye on someone who does that activity well. Remember that the scanning step is the opening of the door to your mind. The wider the door is opened, the more you will be able to take in. As you observe more, be sure to stretch your mind to seek to explain and relate.

At times you may want to direct your scanning toward specific areas where you want to know more about something. You may want to read about some new subject which is apparently relevant to your job. You may want to understand a person better; you can take a step in that direction by scanning the information already available to you—what she does, what she wears, what she chooses to display on her desk at work or in the rooms of her home, what she chooses to talk about. Usually, people don't even begin to capture the information readily available to them.

The importance of scanning is to keep a wide range of knowledge available to you. It will fuel your creativity, enhance the experience-base for your discernment, and provide you with alternative choices of subject matter on which to focus in your interpreting and organizing.

2. ASK.

As you scan, ask yourself which subjects are worth further analysis. Perhaps your initial observations and interpretations arouse your curiosity or show that you have a need to know more. As you sense this, decide to focus. The point of this step is to encourage you to make this a little more of a conscious decision concerning the added expenditure of your time and mental energy.

What is relevant for further focus varies according to your need, interest and perspective. Most of your daily choices are routine. If you are looking for a place to eat out, you naturally focus on each restaurant, thinking through what is available there, the price of its food, and what is appropriate attire for dining there. You compare each of these factors to your desires and circumstances. Sometimes we limit our concept too quickly of what one thing can do. A typical restaurant is also a place which provides pay phones, restrooms, change, travel directions, warmth, gum, and toothpicks to name a few additional factors. Under certain circumstances, each of these items could become important to you.

Sometimes you really need something out of the ordinary. That is when you stretch your mind. In the last chapter we told the story of how a man's car was caught in a Colorado hailstorm. There was another lesson the man learned from that experience: under emergency conditions, some walkways can be appropriate places for cars. You might recall that after the damage was done, he noticed a sheltered walkway near where his car was originally parked. His car could have been protected there. Part of the problem was that he had another solution (the big tree) in mind and didn't look around for a better alternative. Another part of his problem was that he had put a traditional boundary on his mind which said that cars travel on roads—not walkways. As a result he did not consider the better alternative. So, don't limit your thinking.

As you scan, make it your habit to keep asking if what you are seeing is worth looking into further. Is there some way a particular object could be more useful to you? Is there some way you can help a certain person or he can help you? Would it be interesting to know more about that subject? Would it be worth it to read that article or book? Could your mind be meaningfully challenged by solving that puzzle? Do you have a sense that you should focus?

Keep asking!

3. FOCUS.

When you have determined that something is worthy of further interpreting and organizing, then focus your mind on it. Dig in. Really analyze. Come to some thoughtful conclusions. Apply it to your life. Be able to explain it to others.

For explanation purposes let's consider interpreting and organizing separately.

Interpreting

Remember that interpreting is explaining — determining meaning. In the next two chapters we will relate this more to words and other language-oriented communication. In this chapter we are mainly considering physical objects. So, the question becomes, how do you focus on interpreting the meaning of such things?

Let's again use the six questions to help us focus:

Who?
What?
When?
Where?
Why?
How?

This is a familiar series of questions. But instead of scanning, as under the first point, let's dig in. If you were studying to be a journalist you would make them part of your moment-by-moment thinking procedure. The problem is that most people don't use them regularly and systematically. Very few people push them to the extent we will be sharing with you in what follows.

First, let's look at "Who?" In this case the questions all apply to the relationship of the subject to other people, even though not all of the questions begin with "Who. . .":

"Who is involved in this directly?"
"How does/can this apply to or affect you and your life?"
"How does/can this apply to or affect others?"
"Who caused this?"
"Who benefits from this?"
"Who is interested in this?"

Second, let's look at "What?" In observing, a person would ask the question, "What do I see?" In interpreting he would ask the questions:

"What is it?"
"What are its objectives?"
"What does it accomplish?"
"What is its usefulness?"
"What is its meaning?"

Third, let's look at "When?":

"When did/does/will/can it happen?"
"When does it do that?"
"When is it useful?"

"When does it move or change?"
"When was it made/developed/discovered?"
Fourth, let's look at "Where?":
   "Where is it?"
   "Where did/does/will/can this happen?"
   "Where is it most useful?"
   "Where does it work in different ways?"
   "Where was it made/developed/discovered?"
Fifth, let's look at "Why?":
   "Why does it exist (for what ultimate purpose)?"
   "Why is it here?"
   "Why does it work that way?"
   "Why are those people involved?"
   "Why are its objectives important?"
   "Why would I want to benefit from this?"
   "Why does it change or move?"
Sixth, let's look at "How?":
   "How does it work?"
   "How does it move?"
   "How does it change?"
   "How does it become useful?"
   "How does it accomplish its objectives?"
   "How does it have meaning?"
For interpretation, "how" is crucial. It can be interpreted in light of function, or purpose or size.

As you can see, there is more to each original word than initially meets the eye. Furthermore, none of the above series of questions exhausts the alternative questions that could be asked which are relative to each word. This is just intended to give you the idea of the range of questions and to get you started in the digging process.

Realistically, you normally are not going to ask more than 30 questions about each item on which you focus. Some of the questions make more sense than others under particular circumstances.

Let's build on one of your assignments from the previous chapter and see if we can make these questions practical in a specific setting. Either sit where a guest would sit in your living room or place yourself in a guest's position in another person's house. Ask some of these questions about some specific things you observe and draw some interpretations from your answers.

Let's have Steve take us through an example in his house. A guest sitting in his living room, facing the fireplace, would see a dried floral arrangement on a table in front of him and a large picture of a floral arrangement hanging above the mantle piece. What do these floral arrangements accomplish? Well, they have beauty, they give a slight outdoor or nature setting to the room and they brighten the room.

How do they become useful? They must be displayed tastefully. When are they useful? Basically year-round, although the table arrangement seems more appropriate for fall in light of its deep red, gold and tan colors. Where are they most useful? Displayed, but not in the way of conversation. Who is involved? Judy. She is the one in the family with the flair for plants, flowers and decor.

Why are they there? This question begins to drive you toward some conclusion about Steve and his wife. The flowers seem to be there to create a positive influence on the decor and spirit of the room, which, in turn, positively influences those who are in the room. A guest in their living room might glance around and notice pictures of plants and outdoor landscapes. He would see three live plants in different corners of the room and a vase of cut roses.

By this time, he definitely would be getting the idea that Steve and Judy like plants and the positive, natural atmosphere which plants create in a room. If the visitor noticed the colors of the furniture, walls and carpet, he would see browns, greens and golds. These also are colors related to earth and plant-life.

If a guest had asked the questions we proposed, he would likely have arrived at some answers and would be properly interpreting Steve and Judy's intentions. The guess is, though, that far fewer than half of the people who visit their house even consciously notice these facts and specifically draw any conclusions. Most people probably gain an intuitive sense of the atmosphere of the room without specific analysis. Some people, no doubt, view it as just another living room. Where they focus their attention is, of course, their choice. Some of the people who are least observant of the items in the room may well, by contrast, be the most attentive to what Steve and Judy say in conversation. But the facts are there for anyone to observe and interpret.

Try this yourself. Deliberately focus on aspects of a room that you would not normally notice too much. Push toward some conclusions. If you feel the freedom to ask people about their purposes in their room decorations, do so. Many will be amazed and complimented that you noticed. Some may not even specifically realize what atmosphere they have created for their guests.

Next, try focusing on something else. Find some physical object with which you are not too familiar. Run through the questions above for this object. Try to select something in which you are interested or about which you might need to know more. You will be amazed at how much more there is to interpreting something than initially "meets the eye."

Organizing

Next, as the second part of the "focus" point, let's consider "organizing." Remember that organizing is relating—discovering connections between concepts. This process involves some discernment and creativity. There are many more ways to relate things than most people imagine; so, a person must exercise a certain amount of common sense in choosing organizational concepts for his mind.

Connections have patterns. For example, you can connect concepts on the basis of an objective or purpose. An automobile and motorcycle can be thought of as having the same objective: transporting people. You can also connect concepts by common appearance such as two blond-haired people. You can connect concepts on the basis of meaning. (For example, boat, ship, vessel and craft are synonyms.) The following is a list of some reasons for connections:

Objectives (also purposes, goals, usefulnesses, effects)
Meanings (also significance, connotation)
People (e.g., his, theirs)
Physical characteristics (e.g., shape, color, texture, smell)
Sequence (e.g., first in a list)
Time (e.g., past, present, future)
Parts of whole (e.g., hand, arm, shoulder as parts of the body)
Methods of operation (e.g., makes a certain noise)
Location (e.g., from the same home town)
Experiences (e.g., fought in World War II)

It is not easily possible, nor probably useful, to catalogue all reasons for connections. There are many. Any characteristic of something is a basis by which it can be compared to something else.

Depending on how you choose to organize your observations

and interpretations, you may even see totally different things. One illustration of this is a black and white drawing which you have probably seen. By organizing the picture in one way, you see an old woman. By looking at the picture differently you see a young woman. It all depends on your organization of the facts which you see.

A very important additional point is that contrasts or opposite connections can be made as well as similar comparisons. For example, the cars on different sides of a two-lane highway have a commonness in that they are on the same highway, but they are different in regard to their direction of travel.

We tend to do a lot of our "organizing" subconsciously. We connect people's first names with their last names. We join people together as a family. We recognize many different shapes, colors and sizes of vehicles as automobiles. We connect cities with states, books with authors, and eating utensils with a certain drawer in the kitchen. This connecting capability is crucial to living life; we literally couldn't find our way home without it. The problem is not that we don't do some of it, but that we don't connect things as much as we could and in many cases as much as we should.

How can you improve your ability to connect concepts and see patterns of thought in your mind? Let us offer a few suggestions.

One good technique is to ask specifically if particular types of connections are present. Consider the following items: cup, glass, plate, oven, carpet, patio, wool sweater. Are there any connections between these concepts with regard to objectives or usefulness? A cup, glass, and plate all help us to eat. A carpet and patio both provide a surface on which we can walk.

Are there any connections of meaning? Cup and glass are somewhat similar in meaning. With regard to people, all of the items are used by people. With regard to physical characteristics, the oven, carpet and patio are usually all flat on top; the carpet and the wool sweater could have a similar texture.

Another technique is to think back in your experience for similar items or circumstances and see how they compare to this one. For example, if your car motor turns over very slowly when you try to start it, your experience tells you that the battery is probably low. If you have had much experience with cars, you might also relate a low battery charge with a problem in the battery or the charging system (alternator, voltage regulator or belts.)

Another technique is to ask yourself consciously, "What have I learned that tells me something about this?" Steve has a bachelor of science degree in electrical engineering. In the course of his studies he had the occasion to take quite a number of math courses. Recently, someone called him and asked his advice on how to solve a particular algebraic equation. The caller couldn't seem to get it to work out. Immediately, two facts came from Steve's memory. First, this person is good at working with figures and is persistent enough to have already found any addition and subtraction kinds of mistakes. Second, from Steve's extensive schooling in math he remembered that often the hardest part of solving something is to put it into an equation from words and concepts. That led him to say almost immediately to the person, "I'll bet that problem is in the initial reduction of it to paper." As it turned out, that was true. Once they hammered out the right initial equation, the ultimate solution came quickly.

This illustrates another technique — making assumptions. To start thinking down the line, sometimes you need to make assumptions. Steve assumed that the person mentioned above had not made an addition and subtraction kind of mistake. It was a reasonable assumption, and it took him to the next step of reasoning.

Sir Arthur Conan Doyle created the fictional character, Sherlock Holmes, to be a master of synthesizing reasonable assumptions in light of available evidence. He sets an excellent example for us in how much can be reasoned from very little.

Another useful technique is to learn how to employ your subconscious. According to Bob Dudley, a lecturer with Learning Dynamics, Inc., Needham, Massachusetts, 75 percent of interpersonal communication is perceived at the subconscious level and only 25 percent at the conscious level. No wonder you occasionally have intuitions and "strange feelings." Your subconscious mind has drawn some valid conclusions from what it has perceived and processed, and it is letting you know about it in your conscious mind.

One way to take advantage of your subconscious capability is to feed it the information, then give it time and the right context to mull over the information, which for Steve sometimes involves a short nap. This is explained more fully in chapter 10.

A final suggestion for you on how to organize your thoughts (and in turn, learn) is to point out that there are different natural styles of learning. According to David A. Kolb of Case Western University, there are four basic learning styles. They are listed below with a few of the behavioral characteristics of a person who predominantly uses that style.

Concrete Experience

- likes to let things just happen spontaneously
- enjoys variety, fresh newness, each activity for its own sake
- enjoys the unexpected and changes plans often

Reflective Observation

- hesitates to jump to conclusions
- needs to process all incoming signals and understand the details
- can't be pushed for an immediate decision because he likes to investigate many options

Abstract Conceptualization

- is analytical
- naturally discerns patterns in ideas and situations
- tends to simplify, theorize and draw reasoned conclusions

Active Experimentation

- is pragmatic and goal oriented
- gets an idea then must follow through to see if it works
- may not always think through the implications of an idea in advance

Of course, there are advantages to each approach. People don't tend to use one of the approaches exclusively, although they usually do function more naturally with some than they do others.

Two actions are important here. First, identify the natural tendencies you have and view them as strengths. Build on those strengths. If you tend toward reflective observation, be sure to gather sufficient information and give yourself time to reflect before you must respond. If you tend toward active experimentation, seek ideas with practical application and set aside the time and effort to try them out.

Second, recognize that there are other ways to learn. Don't get impatient with people who don't do things your way. They may observe, interpret, and organize in ways that will bring out insights you won't see. Ask people who use different analytical approaches what they think about things you are thinking about.

As you encounter things today (and from here on) make more of a conscious effort to organize your thoughts, specifically looking for relationships that are not immediately apparent.

4. EXPLORE.

Dig beneath the surface of the information that is readily available to you. If it is appropriate, become an active participant in the environment of what you are considering. Interpreting and organizing are a little like panning for gold. You have to keep scooping up more mud and putting it into the pan. Then you need to wash away the dirt in order to uncover the gold flakes. No new raw materials means no new gold. Similarly, no new information or fresh approaches also probably means no new insights.

Exploring means going beyond exclusively mental activity into inquiry and experimentation. What else do you think you need to know? Where and how can you obtain that information? What can you try? Who can you ask? What can you read?

As you interpret and organize, how can you be more aggressive in pursuing knowledge? Of course, as you dig, you need to honor God and be tasteful with people. So, pray for God's creativity in your seeking and experimenting.

SUMMARY

In summary, interpreting is explaining, and organizing is relating. It is best done when we pray and concentrate on it. The process of interpreting and organizing involves four steps:

1. Scan.
2. Ask.
3. Focus.
4. Explore.

This process is very demanding of our discernment and creativity. As we dig in and focus on a particular concept or object, we must balance being systematic and intuitive in a way that fits the situation and our natural strengths as people. We need to learn to be aggressive in our thinking in order to push beyond the obvious.

Most people don't push themselves mentally and, therefore, they don't make the most of their minds. If you want to improve in this area, you must take specific, conscious action. As an application of the content of this chapter, think back and mull over what you have learned. Be sure to do the personal application and other thinking and action plans called for in the material below.

— — —

I. PERSONAL APPLICATION

What is your highest personal priority application point found in the principles presented in this chapter? Enter that point in the indicated place in the Personal Application Worksheet at the end of the book. In the column next to that enter some specific plans to help you start implementing that point.

II. THOUGHT QUESTIONS

1. In what ways are the four steps of the process of interpreting and organizing different in application from the same four steps in observing? (Scan, Ask, Focus, Explore)
2. Now that I've read how Campus Crusade's Canadian basketball team defeated the Soviet team, can I think of something in my own life where similar observations of details might show me a way to "win" in a tough situation?
3. What six one-word questions will help me focus my interpreting? Do I have the habit of asking those questions? If not, in what ways can I form the habit?
4. What benefits have I experienced when I have been especially "aggressive" in my mental concentration?

III. ACTION PROJECT

What is one thing that you do not currently understand well and about which it would be very helpful for you to understand more (e.g., automobile repairs, home computers, finances)? Seek to learn more about this subject; apply the concepts in this chapter in the process.

IV. FURTHER STUDY MATERIALS

For more information on interpreting and organizing, you will want to consider the Further Study Materials for this · chapter listed at the end of the book.

8

LISTENING

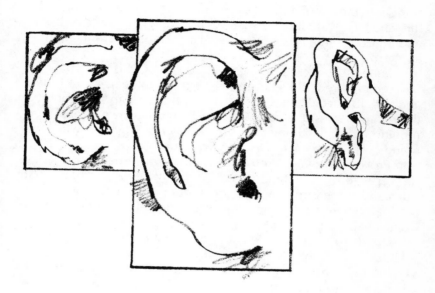

Some time ago, a friend of ours recounted the story of how he proposed to a certain young woman. After the proposal, her response started with a long pause, then the word, "Well," then another long pause, and finally a very weak, "yes," accompanied by a concerned look. He thought that reply to be a total acceptance, and he began to make plans and tell others of his good fortune, only to have his would-be bride break off the engagement in a matter of weeks.

You see, she had never totally agreed to marry him. The point is that he was too biased and wasn't really listening. She was such a gracious person, she had a hard time telling him that she would like to wait and think about his proposal for awhile. The story has a happy ending in that the couple did eventually marry. But this young man could have saved himself considerable embarrassment if he had not allowed his initial enthusiasm, hope and expectation to overrule his normally good capability to listen carefully and accurately.

Yes, how well we listen does make a difference in life. Jesus said in Luke 8:18, "Therefore take care how you listen." Jesus is sharing some parables here and it seems He is suggesting to people that they should not just listen casually or passively, but should be careful and diligent in their listening, because what is said will definitely apply to them.

In James 1:19 we see the wise admonition, "This you know, my beloved brethren. But let everyone be quick to hear, slow to speak and slow to anger." James goes on to say that we can better achieve the righteousness of God if we do this. Another benefit of this admonition can be summarized in the saying, "You can win more friends with your ears than with your mouth."

In Proverbs we find, "And the ear of the wise seeks knowledge" (Proverbs 18:15b). "Listen, my son, and be wise" (Proverbs 23:19a).

It stands to reason that we learn a lot more when we are listening than when we are speaking. Speaking certainly has its place in life, but one of the real keys of knowledge and wisdom and understanding is to learn how to listen well and often.

Unfortunately, we don't always do that. In Matthew 13:14 Jesus says, "And in their case the prophecy of Isaiah is being fulfilled," which says, "You will keep on hearing, but will not understand; and you will keep on seeing, but will not perceive."

Probably the classic example in Scripture of someone who was not willing to listen with understanding was the Pharaoh who was confronted by Moses in Exodus, chapters 8-10. At some point after each of the ten nasty plagues the Scriptures record that the heart of Pharaoh was hardened. He would not *listen* when Moses said on behalf of God, "Let My people go, that they may serve Me." Certainly after the first plague Pharaoh had reason to believe that there were consequences to his failure to listen, and yet his heart continued to be hardened. Now, to be sure, God in His sovereignty allowed (and even enhanced) the hardening of Pharaoh's heart. Yet it would appear that God only needed to extend an already existing attitude.

Yes, listening is truly more than what meets the ear. It is a comprehensive process involving our ears and eyes and our minds and our emotions. Our listening effectiveness increases dramatically for the first few years of our lives, but then about age five it begins to reduce as we learn to obtain more knowledge from reading. We also learn how to listen more selectively to the various sounds that are impinging on our ears. As a result, by the time we are adults we listen at about one-fourth of the effectiveness that we might have as human beings. This is aggravated by the fact that once we learn to talk we have an intense interest in hearing what we have to say as opposed to what others have to say. Perhaps we would be wise to take a tip from how we are constructed physically—our ears weren't made to be shut, but our mouth was.

Listening really helps us live better. In addition to allowing us to be obedient to God's commands mentioned above, and to be more knowledgeable, it also allows us to express our love for people. Through the years both of us have counseled people on many different subjects. Perhaps more important than the specific advice that we would give them is the fact the we really listened to them. In many cases, people mainly want to be heard and feel loved.

Another very important benefit of listening is that it assures us that we are accurately perceiving what a person is saying and thus are able to respond appropriately. So often in conversations people are talking *at* one another, not *to*, making presentations of their point of view rather than taking the time and effort to listen carefully to what is being said by the other person. Proper listening allows customing of remarks to respond to what was said, and to be relevant to that.

Steve has discovered that if he paraphrases what was said to him, he can prove to the speakers that he has heard them. If he then needs to respond in such a way that is not totally in agreement with what they have said, they at least know that the problem is not that he has not understood them. That puts them in a much better position and develops in them willingness to consider what he might say in contrast to their point of view. This is a very important benefit of listening carefully.

Preliminary Steps

Knowing how important it is to listen, let's learn *how* to listen. As with observing and interpreting and organizing, listening starts with two important steps: prayer and concentration. As mentioned earlier, we need to start with them and we need to keep applying them as we think.

Without the supernatural assistance of God, we can never hope to become adequately sensitive to the needs and concerns of other people. Their trains of thought and the subtleties of what they are seeking to express are very often beyond simple human comprehension. Many times Steve has gone from a conversation and then felt the prompting of the Spirit to go back and address something that had not even occurred to him at the time. Sometimes he feels impressed to apologize for something he may have said or to be more sensitive to something that he didn't initially see.

As with the other mental functions — concentration is also key. Many people view listening as a passive activity and speaking as an active activity. When we are listening we think we can sit back and relax and basically turn our minds off. As a result many people don't really listen.

In many ways listening is more difficult than speaking. When a person is speaking, he at least has to know only one subject, focus on that and seek to convey a message about it. When a person is listening, he needs to be prepared and sensitive to whatever the other person might be saying, and if there are others in the room, what they might be saying as well. Furthermore, since he does not know all of what is going to be said yet, he has to observe, interpret and organize what is being said. As you well know, people don't necessarily get right to the point, start with the topic sentence and proceed with a clear outline as they present what they are saying.

When he leads meetings of people in the course of his work, Steve considers it to be a very demanding full-time task. He considers himself responsible for keeping track of the discussion's thread of thought, and for noticing where different people are in terms of their opinions on the subject at hand. He must also draw their opinions into the discussion. Furthermore, at times when the meeting does not seem to be as fruitful as it should be, he needs to take an active role in altering the course of discussion or accelerating it. In order to know when to do that, though, he needs to be listening carefully.

Art Linkletter, perhaps the nation's most successful radio and television host, spent years talking with the most difficult group of people to interview: children. Yet, Linkletter was so good at his job that millions of people watched for years as he drew remarkable truths from his small interview subjects.

In his book, *How to be a Super Salesman*, Linkletter declares, "I suppose one key to my success as an interviewer in radio and TV has been sympathetic, encouraging, thoughtful listening."[1]

He practiced looking the child in the eye without glancing around, never seeming shocked or amused and never demeaning the child's replies, but staying on his level. This caused the child's focus to be exclusively on Linkletter. The result was that the child talked naturally.

In his book, Linkletter advocates the same practice with adults, and urges his readers to try it. We would agree. Listening requires you to be attentive. Lean a little forward mentally. Think of yourself as an active participant in the communication process, being as responsible for communication occurring as the person speaking.

The Process of Listening

As with observing, interpreting, and organizing, the basic process of listening can be summarized in our familiar four steps:
1. Scan.
2. Ask.
3. Focus.
4. Explore.

There are many specific details about listening that differ a little from the other processes mentioned. At the same time, the basic thrust of what needs to be done is the same.

1. SCAN.

This is the normal mode of listening. It is a little more relaxed than the "focus" step, but you still need to be attentive. Imagine your mind operating a little like a radar antenna that you have seen on the top of a ship's rigging or at an airport. The antenna is turning around, sensing what is going on in all 360 degrees around itself. It is picking up various objects out there and then moving on to something else, picking up the presence of other objects. When it comes around the full circle, it's once again where the first object is. It is the beginning of the "tracking" process. In this stage you are observing, interpreting and organizing in the preliminary stages.

The first things that you should be noticing, of course, are words that are being said, what meanings they have, what subjects they seem to be conveying. It is helpful to be looking for the apparent object of the conversation. It may be just to have a friendly chat or some small talk, but whatever it is, it is easier to put the particular words, sentences and paragraphs into context once we know where they are leading.

Crucially important at this (and every other) stage of listening is realizing that most of the content in interpersonal communications is not in the direct meanings of the words said. We could both be wealthy men if we had one dollar for every time someone said to us, "He said he would do it!" by way of explaining why something was not done. The person had earlier asked someone to do something and believed that person said he would do it. The question is, did he give any indication about how excited he was about doing it? Did he indicate when he thought he might get it done?

Did he seem at all concerned or even upset at the assignment? Were there any other indications of something less than an unqualified acceptance?

When it comes to conveying emotion, body language must be considered. People often give us far more evidence by their faces, postures and hands than they do by words. Think of the last time you were around someone who was really angry. What were some of the ways you knew that was true, besides the actual words they said? Probably one evidence was that their facial expression altered, their mouth changed shape, and the eyes seemed to focus sharply. The facial skin flushed. The body probably became tighter than before. The angry person may well be leaning forward in his chair or where he is standing. The fists may be clenched, lips may seem more tightly pursed. Breathing will probably quicken. Words tend to be either measured or blurted out. In any case, the words will be different from what they would be in a more relaxed conversation.

What we have just described are characteristics you would recognize as expressing anger. However, there are many other basic attitudes or emotions that a person can be expressing to you. Those are quite apart from the precise words that they are choosing to say. If you find you have difficulty sensing that kind of evidence, it would be very good for you to take a listening course such as that offered by Learning Dynamics, Inc. Or you may want to read a book such as *Body Language*, by Julius Fast. You will be handicapped in your ability to listen if you are not able to discern non-verbal communication fairly well.

As you are listening in the scanning stage, start to put what is being said in the context of the individual person who is speaking. Certain people tend to communicate in certain ways. One of the evidences that something is more important than usual (or there may be some special emotion involved) is when they deviate from their normal method of expression. Some people are normally very calm and when they become excited, that's evidence that special attention needs to be given. On the other hand, other people would get that excited by just a normal communication.

At this stage you may choose to take notes if it seems appropriate. If you are in a meeting, you can stay more alert by writing down some observations and maybe some key questions you might want to ask.

If you can, begin to put yourself in the other person's shoes. This is called empathy. Occasionally, see if you can paraphrase back in your mind what the person is saying. This may seem like a very easy thing that all people would do well. Yet Steve was in a meeting once where he heard a person make a fairly simple expression to the fact that he *never* thought one particular activity should be viewed as a means to an end, but rather should be an end in itself. Then he heard the person to whom the first person was speaking turn right around and say, "Yes, I agree. It should really be a means to an end." The second person was not listening to the first person at all. He was certainly not paraphrasing what the other was saying, when he said, "yes".

One particular thing to look for at this stage is "selective listening." When his children were teenagers, Lee was a very busy newspaper editor and publisher. One time his son exclaimed, "Dad, you care more about that old newspaper than you do me!"

Lee was hurt. He told his wife, "I thought I was being a good father."

His wife, Cicely, wisely reminded him, "You don't always listen with your heart. You only hear the words; you've got to tune in to what they are thinking."

His teenage son was feeling the loss of his father's time. Lee was so busy with the business of making a living that he wasn't listening to his son's understandable desire for more attention.

Cicely, on the other hand, was listening much more comprehensively to what their children were saying. She was more available to them. When they were dating, she always waited up until they came home. As a result, she helped guide them through the trials and uncertainties which were a part of growing up.

Lee declares, "Cicely's availability to listen was a major contribution to rearing two of the finest kids I know, if a father may be forgiven for saying so."

2. ASK.

As you are in the scanning process, you should be looking for main points the people are making. Watch for ways in which they highlight what they think is important. Also, think of the things that are particularly important to you. They might be saying something in a very casual manner that has tremendous significance to you and is worthy of your focus.

Keep looking for the apparent object of the conversation. If you can discern it, you can highlight the main points more quickly and accurately.

You need to be asking yourself constantly if a particular point that is now being mentioned is a point worthy of further focus. If it is, you then need to move onto the focus step.

3. FOCUS.

When you determine something is worthy of more of your attention, mentally lean forward. Let your radar antenna zero in on that particular region of the horizon. Start discerning what is coming your way.

Many of your listening situations do not lend themselves to taking written notes. But if you are in a situation where you can, without offense, do so. Most people are complimented that you want to pay that much attention.

Steve has been a real advocate of that among his co-workers at Campus Crusade for Christ. It dawned on him one day that his lobbying had borne fruit. Five people were meeting with one person who was not a member of the ministry. Each of them came in and slapped an 8 1/2" x 11" yellow pad of paper on the table as he sat down. The outsider was startled and asked if this was part of the "uniform" of the ministry.

You may want to divide your note pad into three parts according to the types of things you are looking for: key points mentioned, your analysis of what is being said, and questions to ask.

When taking notes, sometimes Steve will draw arrows from one point to another to explain to himself the flow of what is being said. This begins to give him a visual organization of what is being said.

In your notes, be sure you have become aware of (and have written down) the person's objective for the conversation. This becomes crucial for understanding what is being said. Keep asking yourself, "Why is he saying this or that?"

Look for evidence of the person's true feelings and values. They will provide a good indication of how you will be received when you respond in certain ways. For example, an experienced salesman once told of a meeting he had with a customer. The customer rebuffed all of the salesman's approaches by saying, "You're too high! That's too expensive." The salesman looked around the customer's office and saw many very high quality pieces of furniture and decorations. He turned to the customer and asked, "Do you normally buy low priced items instead of high quality ones?" The customer said, "No." "Then let me tell you," said the salesman, "about the many quality features of my product." Eventually he got the sale — because he was sensitive to what the other person valued.

Definitely keep your eyes, ears and heart open for the non-verbal communications as well as the verbal. They may become the essence of the communication.

As you are listening, with focus, start filling in the blanks. Start synthesizing what background might lead the person to come to the conclusion he has. This will prepare you for good identification with a person and his point of view. In fact, we find it very helpful to be able to say (and mean), "I can understand how you have come to feel this way in light of. . . ."

Start putting down questions that you would like to ask when the opportunity arises. Start jotting a few notes to yourself on things you might say in response. Start generating the other side of the story, if there is one. Steve has found that we all tend to view things in a biased fashion. It is good to maintain a little objectivity, while seeking to understand where the other person's views are drawn from. In Proverbs 18:17 we find, "The first to plead his case seems just, until another comes and examines him."

Recall what you know on the subject being discussed. Where does this fit? Is there anything you would especially like to know that you can ask? Does what you know lead you to some interpretation of what is being said?

For example, Steve listened to about 30 minutes of a particular movie on television some time ago while waiting for his flight to be called. As he listened to the TV hero narrate an experience, Steve began to pick up a bias. The person who wrote the script had a very obvious political point of view which strongly colored the perceptions he penned for the hero. Steve could sense that as he contrasted his own observations and interpretations with those of the hero.

See if you can think of direct comparisons or contrasts in your thinking. Are there any of your real life experiences that come to mind? Are there any experiences you have been told about?

Most important, ask if there are any biblical passages which shed light on what you are listening to. The Scriptures, of course, do not provide detailed technical knowledge in many areas. But they do embody God's directives to man for living life. They do contain many, many illustrations of people speaking and behaving wrongly. They ought to be your most fundamental, frequently searched source of information for understanding what you are seeing, hearing, etc.

When Steve is meeting with people in the course of the day, they open and close their time with prayer. Among other things he asks God for wisdom, creativity, solutions, decisions, etc., relative to their conversation. Yet he has found that he can, and needs to, consult with God more than that. As different issues arise, or as he has trouble comprehending what is going on, Steve mentally asks God for wisdom. In 1 Corinthians 2:15-16 we are told, "But he who is spiritual appraises all things. . .we have the mind of Christ." We encourage you to claim that power as you listen.

Fully utilize the concepts you have learned in the earlier chapters of this book, especially concerning how to observe, interpret and organize. For example, the list of interpretation questions under who, what, when, where, why, and how can be very helpful as you listen. Some mental questions you can ask include: What is the usefulness of what is being said? Who is involved, directly and indirectly? Why do things work the way they are being described? How could they work in other ways? Where does this happen and where else might it happen? Review those questions in Chapter 9 often to be sure you are not limiting your interpretations.

A few years ago, Steve was in a group meeting listening to a man who was presenting his thoughts on how a certain area of the ministry ought to be reorganized. Since the man was personally involved in the proposed reorganization, he found it awkward to be too straightforward in the matters that applied directly to him. In the course of an hour, though, he made three indirect references concerning his feelings. The leader of the group didn't notice that and observed that apparently all in the group were in agreement. Since Steve had noticed the above pattern of indirect references, he suggested that they had not reached consensus and proposed that they at least more seriously consider the other alternative. At this point the man did more clearly state his intentions and they had a chance as a group to consider that.

Don't ignore your intuitive feelings as you listen. Since people often choose to be indirect in the verbal aspect of their communication, you can then turn to the non-verbal as a better indicator of their direct feelings. Are they confident or nervous? Are they expecting you to agree or not? Are they emotionally involved in the subject? Often we sense these things much more quickly than we consciously observe them. Therefore, keep your mental ear open to what your subconscious is telling you.

A caution in this area: Look out for your own biases and emotions as they relate to what you are listening to. They can greatly distort how well you listen.

In an earlier chapter we explained some ways to deal with anxiety. There are several good reasons to learn to handle pressure, but one of them is so that you can listen better.

As a final point on "focus", maintain the right perspective of yourself relative to the person you are listening to. You may well have a better comprehension than he does on the matter on which he is speaking. You may even feel he is sinning in some way, but remember, "Brethren, even if a man is caught in any trespass, you who are spiritual, restore such a one in a spirit of gentleness; looking to yourselves, lest you too be tempted. Bear one another's burdens, and thus fulfill the law of Christ. For if anyone thinks he is something when he is nothing, he deceives himself" (Galatians 6:1-3).

4. EXPLORE.

Strange as it may seem, effective listening depends upon the use of your mouth as much as the use of your ears. Exploring from time to time is valuable in observing, interpreting and organizing, and it is especially fruitful in the area of listening. The person on the other side of the table can share a great deal in terms of explanation, if you will only ask.

This leads to the most important part of the exploration process, and that is to ask questions. First, it allows us to gain information on key points. Second, it keeps us alert. Most people can't stay quiet and still track much of what is going on. We have an opportunity to get ourselves mentally a little more "in gear" when we ask a question and then listen to the response. Third, it shows interest in the conversation on our part. Contrast a person who is leaning forward, bright-eyed and frequently asking pertinent questions with someone who is leaning backward with his eyes at "half-mast," not saying a word for twenty minutes. Clearly a speaker would have a sense that he is not communicating. Fourth, the person may be struggling to put a particular concept into words and our questions might help him say what he wants to say.

As indicated earlier, one of the parts of your note pad ought to be sectioned off for questions. In meetings, day in and day out, Steve writes down things that are not clear to him and seem worth asking. He doesn't necessarily ask the question when it first occurs to him. This is a very important point. Some people ask questions incessantly, without reference to whether or not that is a useful part of what is going on at that time. This definitely is not recommended. Keep your questions before you and when it does seem proper to ask, then do so. Also, he hardly ever asks all of the questions he thinks of. He lists by priority the ones that he feels would be most fruitful.

Often Steve finds that a few key questions can make his contributions to a meeting much more precise and helpful. For example, he explains, "In a recent meeting I was called in after the session was well under way and was asked to respond to a particular proposal. I was given an overview of the proposal in just a few minutes. While I outlined the key points of the proposal, I also kept track of some information that I really needed in order to make a valuable judgment. I was then asked to give my recommendation.

"Rather than immediately draw a conclusion, I asked if it would be possible for me to clarify a few things. After receiving answers to my five specific questions, I was able to eliminate many alternative conclusions, and I could recommend more precisely. As I look back on that conversation I realize my contribution would have been a lot less valuable had I not asked the questions."

Another very important part of the exploration process in listening is to paraphrase your current understanding. Perhaps the most important thing this does is show to the person speaking that you are listening and are tracking with him. In your paraphrase, be sure to mention that you are not just listening to his words, but are sensing how he feels in the matter as well. Most people appreciate that. Paraphrasing also forces you to structure what you are hearing. It makes you articulate it, and that is good for your understanding. A third good thing is that paraphrasing gives the person speaking an opportunity to give you feedback on how well you have understood what is being said.

A friend of ours uses the following approach when he conducts marriage seminars. He has the attending husbands get apart and list ten very important things they want to communicate to their wives, but often have trouble doing. The wives form another group for a similar assignment. Then the two groups get back together. One of the wives is selected to receive one of the items from the husbands' lists. As a typical wife she is then given the assignment of trying to paraphrase back to the husbands what she understands they are trying to communicate. She continues explaining and paraphrasing until they, as a group, say that she has comprehended precisely what they are asking. Then a husband is selected to paraphrase one of the wives' items.

The point of the exercise is that often communication doesn't occur because people don't fully comprehend what is being conveyed. This exercise becomes quite humorous, of course, when husbands and wives begin sharing the things they want to make sure they are communicating.

Lee learned of the importance of paraphrasing early in his newspaper days. He was called upon to write about everything from society items to sports, and from civil governing boards, to police matters. Many controversial issues were involved. As a result, it was sometimes extremely important that he clarify a response from a person being interviewed.

A third very important part of exploring is being encouraging. Part of what you do when you listen is to give feedback to a person. Some of this occurs non-verbally and may affect how the person communicates to you. Before you ever open your mouth and ask a question, you should realize you're already in the exploring process even though you're only thinking about what's being said.

Be especially careful of your facial expression. Lee admits, "I am one of those people who needs to be careful of that since I have a stern face." Sometimes his concentration seems to make him scowl as he is listening or speaking. The first year he taught at a Christian writers' conference, he overheard one student tell another, "I don't want to be in his class! He looks mad!" The next year Lee decided to tell that story to illustrate that he didn't bite. He said he was really concentrating hard and he wanted to convey the right words even though his face seemed to be saying something else. At the end of that particular conference one student said to him, "I know what you really are! You are an M & M candy—all hard on the outside but sweet and soft on the inside."

In addition to your non-verbal response to what people are saying, as you have opportunity to comment, give affirming statements of even sounds such as "Uh-huh." If you have the chance, share a parallel experience that would suggest to the person that you agree or can identify with what he is going through. Recently, Steve was listening to someone tell about losing her mother. He was able to explain to her that his dad had died not too long before and, therefore, he could identify with what she was sharing. The person then proceeded to tell him more, knowing that he was listening and understanding.

If you do a good job of encouraging people you will not only be showing your love, but also be stimulating them to do additional thinking and expressing.

If it's applicable and appropriate, turn the conversation to what God's Word says on a particular matter. Often, conversations will not have any biblical concepts in them. But those concepts can be a great benefit in providing solutions and perspective.

In the course of your exploring, and in response to what is being said, you may come to some possible conclusions. Sometimes it is helpful to offer those conclusions in a "trial" form to test the waters for the person's response. This allows you later to lead into a more comprehensive conclusion.

One time Steve was on a plane sitting next to a young woman who was neatly dressed and seemed proper in all respects. In the course of their conversation she indicated she was a fan of a particular kind of family restaurant. She and Steve were sitting in the non-smoking section of the airplane. Putting a lot of these facts together, Steve said, "You don't drink, do you?" She said, "How did you know?" He said, "I was just guessing, but in light of certain other things that you are and think, it seemed like you may well be opposed to drinking."

This area of exploring can be enhanced when you understand more of how to speak clearly and communicate what is on your mind and heart. This will be covered more in a later chapter.

Remember, exploring is a valuable part of the listening process. As a rule, there is no need for you to theorize in a conversation when you can easily ask a question. Furthermore, by actively participating in the process, you assure proper communication—first to you and then from you to others.

SUMMARY

Listening is an important part of our lives, as well as of the functioning of our minds. It is a process in which we need to be active; not passive. It requires a sensitivity to people at the emotional as well as the rational level. It involves observing, interpreting and organizing skills detailed in earlier chapters and applying it in specific ways. As with these other processes, it is best done when we pray and concentrate on it. Also, as with the other processes, its steps can be summarized as follows:

1. Scan.

2. Ask.
3. Focus.
4. Explore.

Most people do not listen very well. Therefore, they don't make the most of their minds, and they don't relate to people as well as they could. If you want to improve in this area, you must take specific, conscious action.

— — —

I. PERSONAL APPLICATION

What is your highest personal priority application point found in the principles presented in this chapter? Enter that point in the indicated place in the Personal Application Worksheet at the end of the book. In the column next to that, enter some specific plans to help you start implementing that point.

II. THOUGHT QUESTIONS

1. Am I the kind of a person who listens actively with my mind, or only half-heartedly with my ears? What evidences do I see one way or the other?
2. James 1:9 says, "Be quick to hear, slow to speak and slow to anger." How can I apply the principles of that verse better in my life?
3. What methods can I use to determine a person's objectives and main content points when he or she is speaking to me?
4. Since listening well includes non-verbal communications, how well do I "listen" to those kinds of messages? What evidences do I see of misperceptions on my part due to this?

III. ACTION PROJECT

Try this: In your next several conversations, make a point of increasing your listening ability. Take notes, discern objectives, paraphrase, and note non-verbals. See what more you learn and see what kind of response you receive from other people.

IV. FURTHER STUDY MATERIALS

For more information on listening, you will want to consider the Further Study Materials for this chapter listed at the end of the book.

9

READING AND STUDYING

Both of Lee's children are avid readers, as are he and his wife. But only in looking back can the Roddys, as parents, see how they taught their children to love books and be motivated to read them. Lee had forgotten one incident until Susan, now in her late twenties, reminded him.

"Dad, remember those little books you used to buy Steve and me? You said we could have as many as we wanted—you'd buy them anytime we asked—providing we first gave you a written book report on the last one you bought us."

Those simple book reports were incentives, not only to read, but to study and enjoy the material. They shaped young lives for good. The attitude was right from parents to children, and no pushing was necessary.

But it isn't always that way. Too often, readers today feel they have been shoved. But reading and studying provide an open door to a fuller life, and the mandate to read is very much a part of the Scriptures.

Jesus expected people of His time to read. In Matthew 12:3, Jesus said, "Have you not read . . .?" In Isaiah 34:16 we find these words, "Seek from the book of the Lord, and read . . . ." In fact, reading was so important that schooling was mandatory for Jews long before Jesus was born. From the works of the famous Jewish historian Flavius Josephus (A.D. 37 – 95?) we learn that universal compulsory education in a Jewish public school system for all boys was started by Simeon ben Shetah. He was the brother of Queen Alexandra. She named her brother as head of the world's first such school and required establishment of at least one school per village. The world's first teachers' college was begun by ben Shetah in Jerusalem so the students would have qualified teachers. Since these Jewish public schools were free to orphans or children of the poor, it seems very likely that Jesus had been educated in this system.

Luke's Gospel tells us that Jesus came to Nazareth after His temptation in the wilderness, entered the synagogue on the Sabbath and "He opened the book [of Isaiah] and found the place. . .and He closed the book. . ." after reading Isaiah 61:1. Later, Jesus wrote on the ground, suggesting His complete literacy.

While compulsory public education has long been required in America, not everyone likes to read. In fact, a literary agent recently said that the entire publishing industry is supported by a mere 15 percent of the nation's population. But it is especially in reading the Bible that many people fall short. The Bible is America's best selling book and has been year after year, yet in a Gallup poll of the general public, 45 percent of those polled could name only four or fewer of the Ten Commandments. Only 12 percent read the Bible daily and more than half (52 percent) did not read the Bible more than one time a month, if ever.[1] And even with the answer supplied in a multiple choice questionnaire, only 29 percent knew that the famous statement Jesus made to Nicodemus was, "Ye must be born again."[2] *The Bookstore Journal* noted, "These two tests reveal the dismally low estate of American biblical knowledge."

If we read God's Word and meditate on it and enjoy it, God promises us great blessing. We will lead fruitful lives and will prosper. One of the reasons is we tend to become in our actions what we think about in our minds.

God details that mechanism for us in Romans 12:2, "And do not be conformed to this world, but be transformed by the renewing of your mind, that you may prove what the will of God is, that which is good and acceptable and perfect." To paraphrase, we stop becoming like this world when we stop making the thoughts of this world our main mental focus. We start transforming to become like God when we start making Him and His ways that main mental focus.

What does this have to do with reading? Plenty! What we read becomes one of the prime sources of material for our thoughts. We recognize the value of reading when we consider that it is the main way we receive the thoughts of people who aren't around for us to listen to personally. Bobb Biehl, a Christian consultant, teacher and author, says that a book is one of the best bargains around. For a small cost you can get an author's best thoughts and experiences on his subject. He probably could not ever deliver that content in person in a more seasoned, careful manner.

Thomas Carlyle once said, "All that mankind has done, thought, gained or been is lying as in magic preservation in the pages of books. They are the chosen possession of men." Aldous Huxley wrote, "Every man who knows how to read has it in his power to magnify himself, to multiply the ways in which he exists, to make his life full, significant and interesting."

Do you want to choose what material you file in the library of your mind? If so, choose to read, and choose to read the right things — those things which will challenge your thinking, inspire your heart and instruct your mind. If you don't, there are plenty of alternative sources which will crash in on your consciousness without invitation and dominate it.

Reading gives maximum flexibility of choice. You can find and read an article or a book in almost any area of your need. More instructional, helpful content is available in writing than in any other form. As Mark Twain once said, "The man who can read and doesn't is no better off than the man who can't read."

This leads us to a serious problem. The average American adult does not read very much or very well. According to Norman Lewis, author of *How to Read Better and Faster*, 200-250 words per minute is the average reading speed of an adult untrained in reading techniques. This is equal to the average speed of an eighth grade student. The average is a little more than 300 words per minute for high school or college students, but deteriorates from disuse in adulthood.[3]

Speed isn't everything. Yet, if it takes many hours to complete even one book, we may become discouraged. We don't tend to pick up the next one quickly. We have only so many hours we can dedicate to reading, even if we are motivated. Why not pack the most enjoyment and helpful content into the time we have?

Perhaps even more important is the need for better comprehension of what we read. Colleges across the country complain more and more about the inability of entering freshman to read. When Steve was growing up in Rockford, Illinois, his friends from the University of Illinois told him of a non-credit English course which was required for many entering freshmen. Some called it "bonehead English." It attempted to upgrade students to minimum university standards in reading and writing.

Yes, reading is important, and most people don't begin to do it as effectively as they could. Reading courses today advertise moneyback guarantees if you do not double or triple your reading speed at an equal or better comprehension level.

In this chapter we would like to expose you to ways to improve both your comprehension and your speed. The basic approach to reading is similar to that of observing, interpreting, organizing and listening. It starts with the preliminary steps of praying and concentrating. It goes on to include scanning, asking, focusing and exploring. In this chapter we have combined them in a single six-point outline. For more ideas on how to do each of these steps, review the parallel step in each of the previous three chapters.

In the focus point, we will show you a simple, widely used technique for studying a particular passage. If you don't have a working study approach in your personal Bible study, this should prove very helpful to you.

How to Read

1. PRAY.

The first and most important step is to ask God for wisdom —

pray. This helps answer some questions such as: What should I read? What should I avoid reading? What are the key insights in the material I will be reading? Are they true and consistent with God's Word? Do they especially apply to me now? Is God intending to use this to cause change in my life? Are there principles that can be shared with others?

These questions are important. As you read, you want to get the most for your time and effort. So ask God for help.

Many times when Steve is studying the Scriptures it seems he is carried by a strong tail wind. Concepts flow as fast as he can write. God is the author of that kind of thinking. It is beyond human creativity.

You may say, "I am really just reading for pleasure and relaxation." Great! Ask God to make it even more pleasurable and more relaxing. In Philippians 4:13, Paul shows us by example that we can do all things through Christ who strengthens us.

2. CONCENTRATE.

Concentration starts with an attitude: "I *will* pay attention to this and I will not pay attention to other things." But it is also aided by a number of actions.

For example, as mentioned in an earlier chapter, be sure to reserve a meaningful length of time for reading and studying the Scriptures every day..Pick a time when you are alert. Schedule other activities around it. If it is first thing in the morning, be sure to go to bed early enough to keep from sleeping through it.

For other reading, keep a number of books handy. That will make it easy to grab one when you have an undistracted moment or want a break between activities.

Set aside specific times in your regular schedule for reading. Form the family habit of having one evening a week where everyone has his nose buried in a book. At the evening's end, discuss what you have read.

Set specific objectives for how many books and articles you plan to read. Keep a list of topics of current interest to you. Look for materials on those topics.

Stretch yourself a little. Don't always read novels or light non-fiction. From time to time, pick a very challenging book or article and let it soak in. React to it.

When you start to read a book or article or passage, set some objectives. What do you hope to accomplish? Pleasure? Learning? What kind of instruction?

Decide to push yourself a little. Try to dig into what you are reading. As you do this, the thoughts you read will begin to displace other thoughts. Before you know it, you will find yourself concentrating. One of the great liabilities of reading too slowly is that your mind is not totally occupied. It desires more material for input and looks elsewhere if the reading material isn't being processed fast enough.

Read books and articles on how to implement other ideas for improving your concentration. Two examples are: *A Practical Guide for Better Concentration* and *Secrets of Mind Power* (see end of book for reference).

Encourage others to read and have them encourage you. Judy is a real example to Steve. Every chance she gets, she reads. Even their daughter, Debbie, before she was two, had picked up the habit. Of course, she couldn't read yet, but she would constantly come up to Steve with one of her children's books and say, "Read the book, Dad!"

3. SCAN.

As you learned in the previous few chapters, it is important to get the big picture before you try to absorb too many of the details. The big picture alone may tell you what you want to know. At least it will give you an idea as to where the many points and illustrations fit in. It may even tell you that you don't want to read any further.

How do you get the big picture? With a book, for example, you start with the front and back covers and fly leaves. They are designed to cause you to read the book, so they tell you essentially what the author will be trying to say.

The next step is the table of contents. It usually is very helpful, with its descriptions and main headings within each chapter. At this point, pause and think for a few minutes. Really try to comprehend the author's approach to the subject. If you haven't established objectives for reading the book yet, this would be a good time. "Finishing" the book may not be your objective. Reading particular chapters of interest may be just right for you. Write down your objectives in a few words.

Next, skim portions of the book you are considering reading. Read the first and last paragraphs of chapters. Read the subheadings in the chapter. Note any key diagrams, highlighted principles or other indications of key points. Mark key points in the margin (if you own the book). Underlining is slow.

Keep up a fast-paced comprehension as you do this. According to Norman Lewis, in *How to Read Better and Faster*, one of the leading causes of low reading speed is "unaggressive techniques of comprehension." Even in the scanning step, focus on absorbing the main points well.

Although much reading content is intended to generate concepts more than emotions, some is just the opposite. In most reading there is some subterranean communication beneath the technical definitions of the words. Look for connotations and attempts to motivate. Without substantially losing your objectivity, benefit from the liveliness and emotion this generates in you. Prescanned materials, such as newsletters, digests and "at-a-glance" resources, can be extremely beneficial, especially, if you are trying to keep up in a vocation or hobby.

Also benefit from book reviews. Do the reviewers recommend reading the book or article? What do they think you would get out of it? Some people even hire others to read and digest materials for them.

4. ASK.

As you scan, ask yourself whether you should focus on one or more of the chapters or concepts you have encountered. Mark in the margins particular application points you want to consider further. Start a set of notes on a separate sheet of paper if that will help you remember. Under these noted points, leave room for future notes. You have begun your outline of the book. But notice that the outline is not strictly of the content itself; it relates to your interests and objectives as well.

As you mark in books and take other notes, you will probably find it helpful to develop your own set of symbols and abbreviations. That saves time and keeps you from losing your pace and concentration.

Always maintain an awareness of why you are reading. Frequently ask if you are accomplishing that objective. If you are reading for pleasure and the book bogs down on you, be aware of that. Skim the next chapter or two to see if things pick up. If not, put that book down and try another one. Don't feel like you must be reading only one book at a time.

To help understand "asking," let's look at why Steve reads the newspaper. Every morning he is confronted with many pages of fresh reading material. Should he read it from front page to back? After all, he has paid for it and news gets stale fast. The answer is, "No." Steve has "asked" many times in his newspaper scanning and has decided on the following points of focus:

1. What is the top news? (This is normally on the front page. In some newspapers there is a summary in a specially marked section in the first few pages.)
2. Is there any local event or person featured that I should note?
3. How did my favorite sports team do yesterday?
4. Are there any good illustrations here for my writing and speaking?
5. Of the things I am currently planning to buy, is anything advertised at a large discount?
6. Is there anything especially humorous which can brighten my day? The comic strips, for instance?

This may seem like a long list of questions to ask every morning. It really isn't. In five to ten minutes Steve can usually answer them. And he never reads the newspaper from front to back. In light of his objective, that would be a waste of time.

Let's consider one other example: mass mailings. If you are very interested in the organization or if you really need the product being advertised, read the piece. If neither is true, then don't read it — throw it away. It was their decision to send it to you, but it is your decision whether or not to read it.

5. FOCUS.

When you decide what is worth your attention, focus on it. Mentally lean forward. Become even more aggressive — "attack" the subject; analyze it; apply it. Mark more in the margin; circle words; take more notes. Take full advantage of the structure you have formed up to this point. Fill in the subpoints. Draw conclusions and applications.

Pause from time to time and take a mental step back from the material. Meditate on it. Give your subconscious a little while to surface key, creative thoughts. Review your notes and where you are in the content. Ask, "Is there any insight I can especially see as I now review the overall outline? Are there some new implications, now that I know more detail?"

Don't feel like speed has to go totally out the window when you focus. You should still push. Remember: too slow a pace can lead to a wandering mind. The techniques for correcting special reading rate problems are beyond the scope of this book. But good books and courses are available to help you in those areas. They are listed at the end of the book.

In the focus step in each of the previous three chapters, there are many additional concepts which will help you gain focus in your reading. Here we would like to add one major study technique to your arsenal. It is a detailed elaboration of a widely used four-point Bible study approach. As mentioned in an earlier chapter, it came to our attention through Dr. Howard Hendricks of the Dallas Theological Seminary.

The main points are:

1. Observe. (What do you see?)
2. Interpret. (What does it mean?)
3. Apply. (What does it mean to you?)
4. Correlate. (Where does it fit?)

This basic Bible study approach can be used for a whole passage, for a verse, or even for a single word. At least some of your Bible reading and study should involve a close look at moderate or short passages. Steve does most of his Bible study that way. But he also uses these concepts in studying material other than the Bible.

The following is a more detailed checklist to help you in your focused study:

1. Observe. (What do you see?)
   ☐ What are the obvious features?
   ☐ What is the theme?
   ☐ What is the context of what you are studying? (This may lead you to reference materials as well as a reading of the entire chapter or book involved.)
   ☐ What is the logic or structure employed here?
   ☐ What are the key connective words (such as, and, but, therefore)?

☐ What appear to be the key words of the verse or passage?

☐ What emotions, conviction, humor, controversy, or drama do you see?

☐ What are the key verbs employed? What are their tenses, moods, and numbers?

☐ Who are the people involved in doing or receiving?

☐ What are the geographical or other physical features involved?

☐ What are the time factors (time of day, time elapsed)?

☐ What repetition or other special emphasis do you notice? (This often requires looking beyond the particular passage you are studying.)

☐ What comparisons and contrasts do you see?

☐ What progressions or sequences do you see?

☐ Do you have any special impressions from God as you have prayerfully been observing?

2. Interpret. (What does it mean?)

☐ What are the obvious meanings of the words involved?

☐ From more digging, what are the specific and precise meanings of the key words? (What are the connotations or shades of meaning of the words employed? If you are able, determine the meanings in the original language.)

☐ Why do you suppose some of these particular words were chosen?

☐ What personal identification can you have with the verse or passage? (For example, can you identify with a particular person in the passage and imagine how he feels or thinks?)

☐ What conclusions can you draw from the logic or other structure in the verse or passage?

☐ What are the meanings and the implications of the emotions, convictions, humor, controversy and drama in the passage?

☐ What actions are going on in the passage and what do they mean?

☐ Who are the subjects and what are the objects of the action?

☐ Why do you think other aspects of the verse are as they are?

☐ Can you generate statements opposite to those in the verse and use that as a further understanding of what is being said?

☐ What are some extensions or projections of the statements that are made?

☐ Can you paraphrase what is said?

☐ What symbolism is involved in this passage? (In Bible study: parables and prophecies.)

☐ Is there a special style employed in this particular passage? (In Bible study: Is this a narrative or a prophetic word from God in a particular or special way?)

☐ What are the meanings of the patterns, repetitions, comparisons and contrasts in the passage?

☐ Is there a way in which you can dramatize the lesson of the passage in your own mind?

☐ What conclusions can you draw from the characters and personalities of the people involved?

☐ Are there hard questions that are raised by the passage? (If so, it is important to ask those questions and seek to answer them. One good interpretative tool is to establish what the objective of the passage is. Oftentimes the questions become easier when seen in the context of that objective.)

☐ Are there other items that you *observed* in point 1 above which you have not interpreted yet?

☐ Be sure to ask God constantly for His special insight as you interpret.

3. Apply. (What does it mean to you?)

☐ What are the areas of potential application of the lessons of this verse or passage to you? (Where does your life not fully conform to the message of the passage? It is usually best to start with immediate impressions from God for areas of obvious application. Sometimes, though, it is helpful to walk through your day in terms of time, place, people, and activity for more subtle and specific application opportunities.)

☐ Is there a previous pattern in God's leading in your life that is strengthened by the lessons of this passage? (Are

you being totally honest with yourself in your evaluation?)
- ☐ How does the lesson of this passage compare to your known strengths and weaknesses?
- ☐ What are the practical details of implementing the lesson of this passage in your life? (How will it be done, and when, and with whom, for example?)
- ☐ How realistic is this proposed approach in light of how you tend to operate? (Can you involve another person in helping you in this area, in praying for you and asking about your progress?)
- ☐ What application does this passage have to other people? (Be sure to wait until you first have had the opportunity to think through its application to you.)
- ☐ What opportunities will you have to teach these lessons?
4. Correlate. (Where does it fit?)
- ☐ From your memory, what other content is related to this (other passages of Scripture)?
- ☐ What other passages are mentioned in the cross reference material available in your Bible?
- ☐ If more referencing seems appropriate, be sure to use special resource tools that are available (concordance, topical Bible, commentary, proper name concordance, books on the topic).
- ☐ Create a list of meanings from other passages of the Bible that would strengthen the principles established in this verse or passage.
- ☐ List various passages of Scriptures that limit how far the principles of this verse or passage could be extended. (For example, law is taught in various portions of the Bible. And grace is taught in various portions of the Bible. They are, obviously, both true points, so the question becomes, how do they relate and how do they form boundaries on each other?)
- ☐ In correlating and absorbing the many lessons involved, simplify the essence of the lesson in order to avoid undue complications.
- ☐ Think through the implications of what has been suggested, particularly the interpreted point, as to how

it fits into other passages of the Bible.
- □ As you correlate, be sure to study the principles in their context. Often, seeming contradictions are quickly resolved with a look to context and objective of different passages.
- □ Assess the degree of emphasis or de-emphasis of a particular point in Scripture. (Some points are one-of-a-kind in Scripture; other points are constantly emphasized.)
- □ Are there any particular impressions that God has given you as you have thought of correlating?
- □ As a final step of correlating, you should have a combination or synthesis of points that sharpen and limit the point you have been studying.

Obviously, there are more questions in the study technique than you can answer quickly. The purpose of the checklist is to give you a number of prying tools with which to dig in and open up your material. Use the questions that are most helpful in any given situation, and don't worry about the rest. Digging below the surface does require work, but it is very rewarding. You will see insights you have never seen before.

In the process, you will become a better thinker. Analyzing reading material is one of the best ways to learn how to observe, interpret and organize. From time to time, go back over the principles taught in earlier chapters and apply them to your reading and studying.

All of this has been under the focus point. Now let's go on to the last point.

6. EXPLORE.

Exploring means to search beyond information that is immediately available. It is the complement to scanning. Instead of looking at something from 30,000 feet in the air, get down on the ground and train a microscope on it. Exploring involves active participation as opposed to passive observation.

The basic techniques of exploring as you read have been built into the previous points, especially in the "focus" step.

The only things we would add here are a few thoughts on study resources that can be of help to you.

Since you don't want to go to the library to answer every question you have, you should have some resource aids in your home. Basic general reading aids include a dictionary, an encyclopedia and a synonym finder. Basic Bible study aids have been listed in the earlier chapter, "Obtaining Wisdom from the Scriptures."

In addition to general study tools, you can locate on library shelves a wealth of material on most topics. As you define your study project, you can tap these resources specifically.

In Bible study, it also can be helpful to use widely available Greek and Hebrew study tools. Steve's personal Bible study has been enhanced by them. It is very helpful to his interpretation to know exactly what was meant by the original word used, as opposed to the English translation. You don't have to learn to speak or read Greek or Hebrew to use much of the material available. On the other hand, with the excellent English translations available today, you can do good observation without that and may not want to invest the time or money which using these materials would involve.

SUMMARY

Reading is a very important part of how we gain information for our minds. It is a process in which we need to be active — not passive. To do it well requires taking the initiative and being aggressive. It involves the observing, interpreting and organizing skills mentioned in the earlier chapters and it involves some new, more specific techniques that can be applied in the reading and studying contexts. As with the earlier chapters, the key points are:

1. Pray
2. Concentrate
3. Scan
4. Ask
5. Focus
6. Explore

Most people do not read and study well. Therefore, they don't make the most of their minds. If you want to improve in this area, you must take action. Think back over what you have learned in this chapter and answer the personal application questions below.

I. PERSONAL APPLICATION

What is your highest personal priority application point found in the principles presented in this chapter? Enter that point in the indicated place in the Personal Application Worksheet at the end of the book. In the column next to that enter some specific plans to help you start implementing that point.

II. THOUGHT QUESTIONS

1. Why is reading important to me? What are some specific tangible benefits?
2. Without looking back at the chapter, can I think of at least five specific ideas that can help me improve my reading and studying habits and skills?
3. Do I read fast enough to meet my reading needs? If not, how can I improve?
4. Which of the books mentioned in the "Further Study Materials" section looks like it will be most helpful to me at this time? Where can I obtain a copy?

III. ACTION PROJECT

Select a non-fiction book on a secular subject of interest to you. Determine which few chapters are the most worthy of your focus. Then apply the four-point outline presented in the "focus" point of this chapter as you seek to study those chapters. When you are through, evaluate how much more you learned than you otherwise would have learned.

IV. FURTHER STUDY MATERIALS

For more information on reading and studying, you will want to consider the Further Study Materials for this chapter listed at the end of the book.

10

BEING CREATIVE

A few years ago Lee was doing research for a book when he discovered the true account of how a railroad bridge was built across the Niagara Falls gorge. The contractor offered a ten dollar prize to the first boy who could sail his kite across the chasm to men waiting on the other side.

The lucky boy's kite string was used to haul across a slightly heavier cord, and that in turn brought over heavier material until eventually steel cable was stretched across the fissure. A railroad bridge was built because of somebody's creativity in using a kite string.

We are creative creatures because we are of God, whom we know as the Creator. In fact, the very first impression we have of God in the Scriptures is that of someone creative. He pushed back the existing boundaries of reality, and created something new. And we're to imitate God. Consider these verses, "In the beginning God created the heavens and the earth" (Genesis 1:1). "And God created man in His own image, in the image of God He created Him. . . ." (Genesis 1:27). "Therefore be imitators of God, as beloved children" (Ephesians 5:1).

The first description we have of man is that he was created "in the image of God". It certainly should not surprise us that man has creativity—not to call new universes into being, but certainly to think of fresh ideas, try new approaches and discover new things. As a matter of fact, we are commanded to imitate God.

What is creativity? We would like to propose the following working definition: "Creativity" is the ability to think beyond existing boundaries.

Creativity is absolutely essential if you want to make the most of your mind. It is good to be able to observe with careful scrutiny, to interpret with discernment and to organize your thoughts with neatness and clarity. And if you do those well you will be far, far ahead of the average person. But to improve things dramatically, take on new challenges, develop and utilize yourself to the maximum, you must be creative. You must be able to think beyond your current comprehension; you must trust God to empower you to go beyond what you are and on to what you can be. Be cautious about coming to conclusions too quickly.

Bill Bright, founder and president of Campus Crusade for Christ, is one of the most creative people we know. One of his favorite imperatives to those around him is, "Let your mind soar!" In this chapter you will be encouraged to let your mind soar from time to time, to reject focus sometimes in favor of flow, to reject limitations in favor of opportunities, to test assumptions rather than make them, to unleash your energy in order to generate the "breakthrough" idea.

The Process of Being Creative

The following are eight steps toward becoming more creative. As you study them, consider how they can help you with that breakthrough idea.

1. Ask the Creator.
2. Arrange a creative setting.
3. Sharpen your objectives and become committed to them.
4. Be open.
5. Harness your natural energy.
6. Stimulate your thoughts.
7. Push the boundaries.
8. Employ your subconscious.

1. ASK THE CREATOR.

Some time ago Steve was in a meeting with several pastors where the objective was adequate follow-up and discipling of the unprecedented number of people around the world who were becoming Christians. The goal seemingly was impossible because of places where there were few or no existing churches. They started the meeting with prayer, asking God to cause them to think of "impossible" ideas to accomplish the "impossible" task and for specific methods that could be applied.

The pastors came up with unique ideas. They thought of combining radio and tapes with visits from mature Christians. New ways were developed to train and equip relatively young Christians to shepherd local groups of believers. Ideas were even developed to overcome a wide range of language and cultural problems. God specifically answered the group's prayers.

Although this meeting's topic was different from that of most of the meetings Steve attends, the procedure and the result were not different. Frequently, the leaders of the ministry of which he is a part (and of other ministries with which he associates) ask God for wisdom for things they have not previously known, and God answers that prayer. They claim James 1:5, "But if any of you lacks wisdom, let him ask of God, who gives to all men generously and without reproach, and it will be given to him." They also claim Philippians 4:6, "Be anxious for nothing, but in everything by prayer and supplication with thanksgiving, let your requests be known to God," and Proverbs 16:3, "Commit your works to the Lord, and your plans will be established." Steve and other leaders believe that means not only that the plans will be implemented, but also that those plans and thoughts will be established in response to the prayer.

It has been their experience that God causes magnificent thoughts to enter their minds. In Ephesians 3:20 we find, "Now to him who is able to do exceeding abundantly beyond all that we ask or think, according to the power that works within us." Just think of how much power God is willing to use within our lives, according to this verse.

First look at the phrase "beyond all." In Greek, that is *huper panta*, which means beyond all things or above all things. Next look at the phrase "exceeding abundantly." The Greek term here is actually just one word, *huperekperissou*. The root of this word, *perissos*, means exceeding some number or measure, over and beyond, more than necessary. *Ek* is the prefix which intensifies the already existing idea of the verb. Thus, to the degree that *perissou* already means to be in excess, *ek* suggests it is even beyond that. The word *huper*, which is another prefix, means above and beyond. So, to translate literally from the original language what is meant in this verse, "God is able to do above and beyond that which is above and beyond that which exceeds measure according to the power that works within us."

A phenomenal amount of power, including knowledge and creativity, is available to us. The verse implies that this knowledge will rise from God's Spirit that works within us. God, the Master Creator, therefore the Master of creativity, offers it to us in measureless quantities. All we need to do is ask and trust Him for it.

2. ARRANGE A CREATIVE SETTING.

The kind of setting that stimulates different individuals varies. It is important that you determine what kind of setting you need. You need to balance the absence of distraction and the presence of inspiration. There are a number of variables you can work with.

First, most people are not very creative when they are either too hot or too cold. For most, the temperature needs to be comfortable or even a little on the cool side to maximize alertness.

Second, with regard to position, experiment a little. Mark Twain could write only when lying down, whereas Hemingway wrote everything while standing. Jack London liked to sit at a large desk, but Frank Slaughter writes while relaxing in an easy chair. President Kennedy, because of back problems, thought best in a rocking chair. "Position yourself" for your own creativity.

If you are going to sit, you need to give some attention to your chair. Too comfortable a chair with a hassock on which to place your feet could well induce sleep. On the other hand, something too stiff or uncomfortable could be a distraction.

Third, control the sounds around you. If noises distract you, do what you must to reduce their interference. Close doors and windows. Turn on a dehumidifer and use its hum as "white noise." Play an FM radio softly as a screen for other noises. Work at the local library or in a conference room when it's not being used. You can find solitude if you really seek it; you can control noise if you work at it.

You, likewise, can use sound for motivation. Inspiring music can get you excited. Mood music can help place your thoughts in a different scene.

Fourth, control the scene. Clutter is distracting; try to remove it. Movement is distracting—pull the drapes; close the door; turn off the television. Do whatever you must so your eyes will not be averted and interrupt your concentration.

Colors play a part in creativity, too. Some colors, such as violet, blue and green, are cool colors and have certain negative aspects for some people. Other colors, such as beige, gold and rust, are warmer and may be stimulating for other people.

Fifth, you must learn to protect your privacy. Intense concentration calls for situations of solitude and uninterrupted isolation. It is pointless to try to gain mental momentum if you expect to be interrupted at random intervals. You need privacy for yourself. Get up an hour before anyone else is awake. Take the phone off the hook when your children go down for a nap. Have your secretary hold all calls from 9 to 10 a.m. Do whatever is necessary to set aside private time for yourself so that you can maximize your concentration powers.

However, a major exception to that is when we deliberately want to put something on our "back burner" and mull it over for a while. In that case, it is sometimes better to do other things, for a time. We need to remember, though, to have some means of recording and capturing ideas that occur to us as they surface to the conscious mind.

As you contemplate the need for special creativity on a particular subject, arrange for the setting that is most conducive to creativity for you. When you find a place that works for you, remember, and "use" it when you need it.

3. SHARPEN YOUR OBJECTIVES AND BECOME COMMITTED TO THEM.

Steve attended a meeting where there had been an extended period of brainstorming regarding a particular problem. But, since the group did not have an accurate understanding of the problem, much of the brainstorming was not relevant. Steve took a few minutes to identify the real problem and its aspects and causes. The subsequent brainstorming resulted in many ideas that were then helpful in solving the problem.

A number of years ago a prominent businessman embarked on a particular business outside of his normal area of expertise. His cause was very noble—the education of Christians—but his approach was not particularly fruitful, and the business failed.

This businessman had not recognized three things: (1) what it would take for the buyer not to be threatened by the product; (2) how to overcome some existing technology problems; and (3) how to keep his product interesting to those people who were using it. Strangely enough, each of these problems had a relatively simple solution; yet, the man had failed to recognize it existed because of the lack of a sharp focus on the objectives.

A second and equally important aspect of having objectives is being committed to them. God seems to provide extra adrenalin when creativity is stimulated by an enthusiastic desire to accomplish a particular objective. Napoleon Hill gives a striking illustration of this.

The morning after the great Chicago fire, a number of merchants stood on State Street, surveying their ruined stores. They debated whether to stay and rebuild or to leave the city and start again someplace else. With the exception of one man, they decided to leave.

Hill declares, "The merchant who decided to stay and rebuild pointed a finger at the remains of his store and said, 'Gentlemen, on that very spot I will build the world's greatest store, no matter how many times it may burn down'."[1]

That was almost a century ago. The store was built. It stands there today, a towering monument to the power of that state of mind known as a burning desire. The easy thing for Marshall Field to have done would have been exactly what his fellow merchants did.

The commitment to the objective does not have to be *initiated* by the people needing the creativity. Napoleon Hill gives another illustration in his book concerning Henry Ford and the V-8 engine. Henry Ford conceived the idea that an engine block could be built with 8 cylinders all in the same block. All of his engineers argued, to a man, that it was impossible to do that. Ford insisted that they produce it anyway. They continued to say it was impossible. Ford authorized them to spend whatever time and money was needed to do it. Twelve months went by and the engineers still had not accomplished the objective, but Ford ordered them to continue to do what they said was an impossible task. Ford said, "I want it and I will have it."[2] History records that shortly thereafter, seemingly as if by a stroke of magic, the secret of putting 8 cylinders in one block was discovered. Henry Ford's own commitment was sufficient to compel the creativity of his engineers.

4. BE OPEN.

If you expect to be creative, you must have a basic frame of mind that is open to new ideas. Some people say, "It can't be done" to almost any idea. They are clearly going to have problems being creative and seeing breakthrough ways of doing things. So don't let that be your frame of mind. Arthur DeMoss and David Enlow in their book *How to Change Your World in 12 Weeks* observe, "One absolute essential to success in life is receptivity."[3]

Success grows out of ideas. As a matter of fact, our very growth as Christians hinges on our mind's ability to be open to the movement of God. In Ephesians 4:23-24, we are instructed to "be renewed in the Spirit of your mind, and put on the new self, which in the likeness of God has been created in righteousness and holiness of the truth."

In his book, *Think and Grow Rich*, Napoleon Hill also declares that the subconscious mind is more susceptible to influence by impulses of thought mixed with feeling or emotion, than those originating solely in the reasoning position of the mind. He goes on to describe some positive emotions and a number of negative ones. Examples of positive emotions include faith, love, enthusiasm and hope. Hill says these are the emotions most commonly used in creative effort.

This has been our experience, too. The creative mind is generally a positive mind. It is enthusiastic and optimistic, looking forward to what lies ahead. (See Chapter 3 for more ideas on good mental attitudes.)

Hill mentions a number of the negative emotions which detract from creativity. They include, among others, fear, jealously, hatred, greed, and anger. These and other kinds of attitudes are both causes of and results of anxiety. They serve as a major drain of your energy that could otherwise be harnessed for creative purposes. They can give you headaches and make you feel depressed and discouraged. (See Chapter 2 for more ideas on handling anxiety.)

In summary, cultivate your optimism and avoid those situations that would cause you to be pessimistic and discouraged. Associate with people who are encouraging and avoid those who are discouraging, especially when you want to be creative.

5. HARNESS YOUR NATURAL ENERGY.

A number of years ago when he was single, Steve had a room-mate named Lindy. He and Steve kept schedules that were pretty much the opposite of one another. Steve was a morning person and Lindy was an evening person. In the morning as he would leave around 7 o'clock, Lindy was just awakening. Of course, Steve had already showered, shaved and eaten and was dressed to head out. Sometimes Lindy would be sleepily emerging from his room dragging his towel toward the bathroom. Steve sometimes thought his cheerful, "Hi, Lindy" had ruined the rest of the day for him.

On the other hand, if Lindy would try to keep Steve interested in a conversation beyond 10 o'clock at night there would be no hope for Steve's intelligent, alert involvement. His energy cycle was at a low.

The point is that each person has his own natural time of high and low energy. Since energy is one of the keys to creativity, the trick is to make the best use of your energy cycle. Schedule brain-storming and other kinds of creative projects during times of natural high energy and alertness. Schedule more routine activities for your slower times.

For Steve's wife, Judy, the best time for her to be creative is just after she turns out the light for bed in the evening. Her mind is such that it becomes hyperactive when all of the other distractions of the day have passed. It is very practical for her to keep pencil and paper at the bedside to record creative ideas that occur to her.

When you do get into a creative period, don't stop if you can help it. When he was working on the original outline of this book, Steve had an extended period where he sensed that ideas were flowing at an unusually fast pace. Although he had some other things planned for particular times of that day, he canceled them so he could continue to roll with this extended creativity period. When he can't seem to write fast enough, Steve gets a tape recorder. Then he can dictate ideas occurring to him and not have to stop. During such times, he does not stop to evaluate or judge his ideas, but simply captures them on paper or tape.

Since creative times are much to be desired, especially in certain kinds of projects, Steve does his best to stimulate them whenever he can. Some people keep pushing on a project even though they become sleepy and the ideas aren't flowing. Steve has found the best thing for him to do at that time is to catch a short nap. Anywhere from 20 to 60 minutes sleep will put him in an entirely different frame of mind. Within 15 minutes after awakening, he can count on at least two highly creative, highly energetic hours.

Thomas Edison was known for his frequent naps. He frequently wouldn't accumulate more than four or five hours of sleep in an entire day, sometimes napping on his desk. He then would arise refreshed and creatively recharged.

If a nap is not a possibility, or doesn't seem best for you, get some exercise or do something to get the blood flowing again. Be sure you get enough overall sleep so you won't be dragging through the day.

Lack of sleep dulls your creativity, and so do heavy meals. A frequent "dead hour" for people is right after lunch. A rather large, starchy lunch takes a lot of the blood away from your brain for digestion. Keeping in good physical shape enhances creativity. A healthy body leads to a healthy, energetic mind.

In short, learn when you are naturally energetic and seek to match high energy periods with times where you need high creativity. Learn to stimulate and prolong these kinds of periods with the techniques mentioned above.

6. STIMULATE YOUR THOUGHTS.

There are a number of things you can do to stimulate creative thinking. Thomas Edison is quoted as saying that genius is 2 percent inspiration and 98 percent perspiration. Don't be afraid to work.

As Steve had gotten some distance down the line on this book, he thought it would be helpful to ask two men to a meeting because he finds them very stimulating to his creativity in this area of the mind. During that meeting Steve turned on the tape recorder, told them a little of what he was planning and asked them to comment. Not only did Steve learn directly from them, but many significant breakthrough ideas occurred in his own mind in response to their ideas.

Whenever you can, brainstorm with people who stimulate your creativity. Read books and articles on the subject on which you need creativity.

Another source of ideas is an expert. Some people are specialists in an area in which you need wisdom and creativity. They should be sought for that purpose. Other people are good general advisors. Another kind of person to involve, from time to time, is someone totally unrelated to and perhaps even without experience in the area for which you are seeking advice. His fresh approach may allow him to break through where established ruts are slowing you down. This is known as the "odd man out" practice. It is so practical and so successful, many Ph.D. candidates are guided throughout their studies by a five person committee — four professors who are in the department the student is studying in and one professor from a completely unrelated department.

Sometimes certain "things" can stimulate creativity. Perhaps, if you are thinking about a particular subject, it would be helpful to bring in certain objects related to that subject. Seeing them, analyzing them and studying them may spark an idea.

Analogy is another technique that is helpful in stimulating your thoughts. For example, in Ephesians 3:17 we find, "So that Christ may dwell in your hearts through faith; and that you being rooted and grounded in love. . . ." The word "grounded" in this passage seems to mean primarily to be very firmly footed on the earth.

As you tackle a particular problem, see if you can think of other situations that are parallel to this one and see what they add to your understanding.

Another somewhat similar approach to this is to think of different unrelated items and then try to relate them. That stimulates your creativity. Think of some item from the kitchen, something from the living room, something from your office, and a piece of clothing. Then say, "How can I relate all these to each other?" As your mind seeks to build new relationships, it breaks out of its former mold.

Another specific technique is to write different ideas that you are seeking to organize onto a number of 3" x 5" cards, one idea per card. Then rearrange the cards in different order so that you are physically creating different relationships between the ideas. That will take you out of the mold of your previous mental outline.

Sometimes you just need to get into the middle of your creative challenge. After some detailed thinking, you need to roll up your sleeves, dig in up to your elbows and get involved. As you get into the situation, your creativity will be stimulated.

Somewhat related to that is one of Steve's techniques for stimulating creativity concerning speeches and articles. One of the best things he can do is commit himself to speak on a particular subject. As he is forced to prepare, his creativity is stimulated. In addition, as he speaks new ideas occur to him. It is, therefore, very important for him to have someone taking notes or to record the talk.

Finally, do not think in terms of all the creativity that you are going to have on a subject occurring at one particular time or with one particular burst of energy. Your subconscious plays a very important role in creativity. And it generally requires time in which to operate. Steve found that one of the best strategies is to stimulate his thoughts by the techniques mentioned above and then to allow some time for them to simmer in his mind. He captures thoughts on a pad, 3" x 5" cards, or a tape recorder. He then schedules another time when he will have another intensive thinking time, and this will benefit from some ideas that will surface in the interim.

7. PUSH THE BOUNDARIES.

The very essence of creativity is an eagerness to push beyond what now exists, to test assumptions, to explore boundaries and to seek to exceed them. Think of the great breakthroughs that have occurred through the years. Almost invariably you will discover that a previous assumption was proved to be invalid. William Carey (1761-1834) proved this point. Carey was a young cobbler in England when he stood up in a meeting of Christians one night and wondered aloud if Christ's Great Commission was still in effect. Carey wondered if it was still possible God wanted people of his century to go back to missionary work among heathen lands. This practice had ceased long before Carey's time.

The presiding minister said, "Sit down, young man! If God wants to convert the heathen, He will do so without any help from you."

The shoemaker sat down, but he didn't give up the idea. Out of Carey's mind came the idea which produced the modern world-wide foreign missionary movement which involves thousands of missionaries from Europe and North America.

Consider where the Coca-Cola Company would be today if drug store clerk Asa Candler had lived with the original thought that a product he bought from a country doctor was only valuable to be sold in syrup form for medicinal purposes. Instead he saw how it could be used as a soft drink refreshment.

Boundaries are certainly useful for us in living day to day, but boundaries sometimes are enemies of creativity. There are some specific things you can do to learn how to push the boundaries you're facing. One is to play the "what if" game. Specifically mention what assumptions you are making in a problem. Then ask yourself, "What if that were no longer true?" In that case, "How would I proceed from here?" Then go on to whatever conclusion you come to. For example, in planning, it is helpful to stimulate people by saying, "If resources were no problem, what would you seek to do?" That allows their minds to soar to new levels. Then it gives them an opportunity to pray specifically and seek to trust God for the necessary resources.

Another approach is to develop what you might call a "why not?" attitude. In a brainstorming meeting a basic ground rule is that no one should criticize any idea. Whenever a person makes a suggestion it should be received with approval or polite silence. One improvement on this is used by Dr. Larry Poland, a person who has specialized in creative endeavors. He has what he calls a "why not?" session. This is a brainstorming meeting in which every idea mentioned is followed by a refrain of "Why not?" from the entire group. A person might come up with an inane idea that has never been thought of before, yet the group is required to respond enthusiastically, "Why not?" The group's affirmation further stimulates each person's confidence and leads to even more creative ideas.

Steve has found that pushing the boundaries of thinking is almost a regularly needed exercise. Often he is in meetings where planning requires considering things that have never been done before. A number of years ago, for example, a small planning group was contemplating saturation kinds of evangelism in the cities. They realized that crusades and door-to-door evangelism were probably not the total answer to reaching the populations. With some extensive thinking and brainstorming, they came up with ideas of using the telephones, literature, television media spots, billboards and other forms of advertising that had not previously been widely thought of as techniques that could be extremely fruitful in evangelism.

8. EMPLOY YOUR SUBCONSCIOUS.

R. G. LeTourneau, one of this nation's most successful heavy-equipment inventors and a man who openly proclaimed to the business world that God was his partner, got some of his ideas while napping. Napoleon Hill tells of a personal experience with Mr. LeTourneau.

One night while flying together in LeTourneau's private plane, the inventor went to sleep. In about half an hour, Hill saw LeTourneau rise up on one elbow, take a notebook from his pocket, make some notes, and return the notebook to his pocket. But Hill noticed that LeTourneau had not looked at the notebook as he wrote; instead he looked into space.

The scene was repeated three times before the plane landed. There Hill mentioned the incident. LeTourneau seemed surprised, "Did I make notes?"

The industrialist pulled the notebook from his pocket and exclaimed, "There it is! I have been waiting for this for more than a month. There it is! The very information I had to have before I could go ahead."[4]

Psalm 16:7 says, "I will bless the Lord who has counseled me; indeed, my mind instructs me in the night." Psalm 127:2 reads, "It is vain for you to rise up early, to retire late, to eat the bread of painful labors; for He gives to His beloved even in his sleep."

Clearly, there is more to creativity and thinking than meets the eye and the conscious alert moments. There is a subconscious element of the human being which is not only reflected in Scripture, but illustrated in the life of R. G. LeTourneau and many others. The subconscious mind mulls over and reflects on ideas and generates intuitive thoughts which later surface to the conscious mind.

As suggested by the above verses, often this is best tapped in sleep. This is probably why people use the expression, "Let me sleep on it and I'll give you my answer tomorrow." During sleep our conscious mind is more dormant. Apparently the quietness and the lack of sensations from the outside are used by God as contacts for causing ideas to simmer in our subconscious. These ideas surface to our conscious minds shortly after a time of sleep.

Steve has certainly found this to be true. One of his best techniques for thinking through a difficult problem is to review all of the facts before he takes that nap mentioned before or before he sleeps for an entire night. This is "loading" the subconscious. When he awakens, he jots down the thoughts that are on the top of his brain. Oftentimes he will find that the solutions will have been resolved in his subconscious mind. Some people have to be careful about doing that, expecially with problems that cause them anxiety. They might not get any sleep.

Let us generalize what has been mentioned above. The best technique we have found to involve the subconscious is to obtain a broad base of exposure to whatever facts are involved and perhaps even to what trial alternatives have been thought of. Sometimes this is a long, slow exposure. Sometimes it involves brief intense sessions of concentration on the matter in order to heighten the emotion, desire and excitement about the idea.

The next step is to allow a time of simmering. This definitely does involve time. It generally is not something that happens in a minute or two. It can take hours, perhaps days, or even months. During that period, the idea might be very much on the "back burner" of our minds. Despite that, though, we have to have a collection of techniques for bringing the ideas to mind later when we are going to be putting them all together.

Steve finds some of the best things to have available are 3" x 5" cards so that when a specific idea comes about he can write it down. Then he puts the cards into files relating to particular creative projects. When the time comes to actually organize a certain project, he may well have had three or four or even ten specific ideas which have come to mind in the interim period. Sometimes, all he needs to do at that point is to organize those thoughts in order to have the main points of a talk. Sometimes Steve finds it helpful to do something in the way of a mini-focus on that particular project, just to draw off whatever is the top of his subconscious. He might do this by talking to someone about the subject.

Remember, it is a matter of exposure for some intense periods of thought, some simmering time and then a collection of those ideas. This could lead to some overall organizing of the thoughts into a good plan.

In the above description, we mentioned the role of emotion and feeling. This is a crucial step in regard to the subconscious, which operates on those things the heart feels are important and need attention. That may not be as obvious to us on the conscious level as it is on the subconscious. But those things about which we are excited tend to fill our minds; they are the things upon which the simmering is occurring; and, therefore, will generate ideas.

SUMMARY

In this chapter we have offered you eight basic ways to be more creative. They are:

1. Ask the Creator.
2. Arrange a creative setting.
3. Sharpen your objectives and become committed to them.
4. Be open.
5. Harness your natural energy.
6. Stimulate your thoughts.
7. Push the boundaries.
8. Employ your subconscious.

As you study these points and consider how they can help you, you'll find that your creative ability has improved. But before leaving this chapter, see how you can apply its concepts in your situation.

— — —

I. PERSONAL APPLICATION

What is your highest personal priority application point found in the principles presented in this chapter? Enter that point in the indicated place in the Personal Application Worksheet at the end of the book. In the column next to that enter some specific plans to help you start implementing that point.

II. THOUGHT QUESTIONS

1. Do I agree or disagree with the following statement: "Structuring your thoughts is the key to creativity"? Why?
2. How important to me is a proper setting for being creative? Where is the place in which I have proven to be most creative?
3. In which of the projects I'm now working on is there the most need to "push the boundaries" in creativity? In what innovative ways can I go beyond what I've considered to date?
4. In what ways can I harness the ideas in my subconscious mind more?

III. ACTION PROJECT

Do one of the following as a means of expressing your thanks to God for what He has done for you in your life:

Draw a picture. Compose a poem or song. Write a "love letter." Give a talk on it to a small group of people.

IV. FURTHER STUDY MATERIALS

For more information on being creative, you will want to consider the Further Study Materials for this chapter listed at the end of the book.

11

PLANNING

Several years ago Steve entered his first 6.2-mile race. He was at the race site around 7 a.m. Do you know what he did first? He didn't warm up, "psyche" up, or limber up. Instead, he walked to a 15-foot long line on the ground with a sign alongside it that said, "FINISH." The runner was hoping to run 6.2 miles, but he wasn't planning on going any further.

Isn't it basic to locate the finish line before starting a race? Who knows where Steve might have run to after finishing that race if he hadn't clearly known where the finish line was?

Yet, how many of us run four hours into the day, or half-way through a project, or 40 years through life, without knowing where the finish line is? Most people don't plan enough. They go downtown to the store and return only to discover there was some cleaning at home they should have dropped off on the way. Some people forget to book a speaker for a meeting until it is too late. Some people get all the way into a major repair project only to discover they didn't bring the right tools with them.

Perhaps most sadly of all, most people basically drift through life.

They go to school because the law requires it and their friends are there. They get a job in order to put food on the table and gas in the car. They get married because everyone else did and they're getting lonesome. They buy a home, join a church, watch TV, raise their children and retire – all because these activities seem to be the "normal" thing to do.

Instead of seeking God's specific direction for these and other courses of action, many people proceed through life without much prayer or thought and, therefore, without God's integrating purpose.

When people reflect on their past, many of them conclude that most of their activities were basically meaningless and worthless in terms of accomplishing God's purpose for their lives. Perhaps they chose the wrong career, or married the wrong person, or settled in the wrong community – all because they didn't listen to God and really pursue His direction.

If you don't know where you are going, you'll probably end up somewhere else, as Dr. David Campbell said in his book by that title. Without a planned objective, you wouldn't know if you had arrived.

In his talk series on goal-setting and success in life, Lewis Timberlake asserts that one of the four main reasons people fail is that they have no goal. He says, "Every great person who lived was a nobody until he had a goal for his life."

Have you ever heard about how the live frog was cooked? He wasn't placed in boiling water. Any half-way smart frog would know enough to jump out of hot water. So, he was placed into cold water – the kind he is used to – and then slowly the water was heated until finally the frog was cooked. The frog never sensed a clear point at which he needed to jump out.

A lot of us are like that frog sitting in the pot of heating water. We never reach the point at which we decide to jump out of our aimless life. Before we know it, we are cooked; we have completed the project poorly; we have missed the opportunity; we are old and have not achieved any objective in life.

Jesus spoke plainly to people who were contemplating the idea of becoming His disciples. "For which one of you, when he wants to build a tower, does not first sit down and calculate the cost, to see if he has enough to complete it? Otherwise, when he has laid a foundation, and is not able to finish, all who observe it begin to ridicule him, saying, 'This man began to build and was not able to finish'" (Luke 14:28-30).

The Apostle Paul said, "Do you know that those who run in a race all run, but only one receives the prize? Run in such a way that you may win. And everyone who competes in the games exercises self-control in all things. They then do it to receive a perishable wreath, but we an imperishable. Therefore I run in such a way, as not without aim; I box in such a way, as not beating the air" (1 Corinthians 9:24-26).

Have you ever said, "I didn't get anything done today?" You must have spent your time doing something, but you probably did not accomplish anything that seemed "productive." Very likely you were interrupted by "urgent" things all day. It is a natural human tendency to be drawn to the urgent, pressing things to do, yet these things may not really be important.

Napoleon Hill probably did the most useful research in history when he analyzed hundreds of well-known men over a twenty-year period. These men included Henry Ford, William Wrigley, Jr., John D. Rockefeller, George Eastman, Wilbur Wright, J. Odgen Armour, F. W. Woolworth, Luther Burbank, Alexander Graham Bell, Thomas A. Edison, and King Gillette.[1]

These men achieved successes in various fields of endeavor. Hill undertook to determine what principles of personal philosophy or personal success had made so many of these men rise from poverty to enduring fame. He found that there were certain common characteristics in all those men. From that, he concluded it was possible for anyone to become successful.

Hill listed "plan" as the fourth of six essential elements necessary for developing desires into fruition.

Planning is one of the most frequently called-on mental capabilities. From the time we awaken in the morning until we go to bed at night, we are constantly faced with things to plan: what to wear; what to do; where to go; whom to see; what to say. Plans help us focus our energies, make decisions and be confident. Time will pass. The question is whether we will make the most of our minds and ourselves by planning properly.

How to Plan[2]

Well, how can we plan, then? The following are the five basic steps involved in developing a plan:

1. Pray.
2. Establish objectives.
3. Program.
4. Schedule.
5. Budget.

An elaboration of each of these points follows.

1. PRAY.

In this step you make sure you are appropriating God's wisdom and vision for the plan. If the plan is not what God intended, you have wasted your time and the time of those with whom you work. Sometimes God will lead you in a very unconventional approach. Imagine Joshua's thoughts when the Lord outlined the plan for taking Jericho (Joshua 6:2-5).

Pray that God will give you a comprehension of what He wants you to do, and the creativity by which to get it done.

2. ESTABLISH OBJECTIVES.

In this step you determine what should be accomplished. You establish a target toward which you and the people who work with you will be directing efforts. You cannot determine very well how much money will be spent or when different steps need to be taken until you have determined what should be accomplished. Yet, to many people, planning is merely filling in a budget form or a yearly calendar.

Your objectives are criteria against which you can measure the effectiveness of your present activities. A clear statement of your objectives should also stimulate new ideas for accomplishing them.

Be sure the objectives of your plan put you in a position where you cannot do the job in your own strength, but where you must trust God for the plan to be accomplished. Then God is certain to receive the glory.

3. PROGRAM.

After determining what should be accomplished, the next step is to decide how it should be done. Here you lay out the necessary steps to go from where you are to where you want to be. You start with one activity, then another, then another, until all the right things are going on. You now have a list of needed activities and the order in which they are to happen.

Be especially sensitive to exactly what needs to happen at the lowest level of the program in order for the plan to succeed. What must each individual do, for example, and what is to be accomplished? Also, be aware that if a plan involves trust in God for success, it must involve God at every level. There will be elements that only God can accomplish. However, be sure to specify the steps you can take and be sure to implement them as your part of the plan.

4. SCHEDULE.

In this step, you determine when the different parts of the plan should be accomplished, and you place the activities of the program stage into time slots on a schedule. Determine when each activity should begin and end and enter on the schedule target numbers or milestones that will measure the progress you can expect.

This is a very important step because it puts your plan in a form with which most people can work — entries on a calendar.

5. BUDGET.

The budget step refers to more than money. Many practical issues are faced in budgeting. You do determine how much money is needed and how this money can be obtained. But you also determine how many people you need and how to recruit and train them, and you consider what other resources will be needed and how they may be supplied. Pray specifically for your entire budget. Don't forget, if God called you to the objectives at the beginning of the plan, He is not going to deny you the needed resources (Philippians 4:19).

An Example of Planning

Let's consider an example of planning using the five points we've learned. Let's say that tomorrow you have a weekly two-hour meeting with your staff. This meeting will involve you and five others; so you have decided it will be worth it to make a plan.

1. Prayer.

Ask God for wisdom and vision.

2. Objectives.

Establish the objectives of the meeting:

a. To inform the staff about recent developments (from headquarters, the sales outlets).
b. To give the staff an opportunity to discuss and make recommendations on key issues.

3. Program.
With regard to objective "a," you determine the following activities are needed:
a. Collect all possible pieces of information including correspondence from headquarters and other field directors, recollections of recent phone conversations, trips, meetings.
b. Select those pieces of information that would be of use or interest to the staff.
c. Read these during the meeting.
d. Give each of the staff members an opportunity to pass on information they feel would be useful or of interest to the others.

With regard to objective "b," you determine the following activities are needed:
a. List the key issues to be brought up for discussion and recommendation:

   Progress on upcoming conference.
   Expansion into new office.
   Progress on work project.

b. Determine the order for discussing the issues. *(Let's assume that you cannot get into the new office until the work project is complete, so it would be best to discuss the work project before the new office. The conference is a long way off and was reported last week, so it should go last if there is time.)* Order of discussion would be:

   (1) Progress on work project.
   (2) Expansion into new office.
   (3) Progress on upcoming conference.

c. Discuss each topic (as time is available) and reach the point of specific recommendations for action. *(You are the one to whom the staff is making recommendations for decisions.)*

4. Schedule.

The activities under objective "a" should take about 30 minutes during the meeting (plus some time before).

After that, 45 minutes will probably be needed for discussion and recommendations on the work project, 30 minutes on the new office, and 30 minutes for the conference. Since that requires 15 minutes more time than you have, the conference will be allowed only 15 minutes.

5. Budget.

No money is needed. *(There would have been if you had bought lunch for the group, but you are not doing so.)* The manpower is the staff and they are already planning to be there. You need a place to meet and you decide your office will do.

Try This for Yourself

No doubt you are facing many projects right now which need to be planned properly. Perhaps you have never really written down a plan for your current job (in the office or factory, on the road or at home). Perhaps you have never really considered what your objectives might be in life. Here are some helpful guidelines to personal planning.

Select some specific area which needs planning. Start by praying. Ask God for His wisdom on the matter.

Next, establish objectives. What exactly do you want to accomplish in this area?

Next, design a program. What steps will it take to accomplish your objectives? Or, what *number one* priority activity can you do to take you all or most of the way toward your objectives?

Next, schedule your work. When should you complete key parts of the plan?

Finally, establish a budget. What resources are needed (money and other things)? From where will they need to come?

When you are finished, congratulate yourself. You now have a much better chance of succeeding in this area. Just be sure to keep the plan in front of you and to get started on it.

If you do plan and focus on your objectives, by God's grace, you will reach them.

I. PERSONAL APPLICATION

What is your highest personal priority application point found in the principles in this chapter? Enter that point in the indicated place in the Personal Application Worksheet at the end of the book. In the column next to it enter some specific plans to start implementing that point.

II. THOUGHT QUESTIONS

1. What is the one thing I would like people to say about me when I've reached life's "finish line"?
2. Have I ever heard someone say, "Planning is a waste of time!" What would I now say in response to that?
3. As I mentally walk through yesterday's activities, how many of them could have used more planning as presented in this chapter?
4. What is the difference between an objective and a program activity? Can I give several illustrations of each?

III. ACTION PROJECT

Arrange a meeting with a friend to plan some project of common interest to you. Explain the five-step outline to your friend and come up with a plan for the project together.

IV. FURTHER STUDY MATERIALS

For more information on planning, you will want to consider the Further Study Materials for this chapter listed at the end of the book.

12

PROBLEM SOLVING
AND
DECISION MAKING

Going to the restaurant with Joe (not his real name) is quite an experience. When he receives his menu, he studies it carefully without participating in the conversation around the table. If the waitress asks Joe to order first, a pained expression crosses his face. He hesitates for a time, orders, cancels that, orders again, then finally closes his menu. As others order, he listens intently and often says, "Where did you see that?" If he likes that, he will change his order again. It is not unusual for Joe to change his order two or three times before the waitress leaves. When the food comes he looks at each plate as it is delivered. When his food is placed before him, sometimes Joe will exclaim, "Oh, I should never have ordered this!"

Does that sound familiar? Most of us have seen it happen. Joe is a very intelligent person. He just doesn't enjoy making those kinds of decisions and, as a result, does not make them well.

Yet, solving problems and making decisions are two of the most common activities of our minds. When we reach our closet in the morning, we must decide what to wear. When we get to the kitchen, we decide what to eat. When we drive, we decide what route to take. When our crying child walks up to us, we try to solve his problem. When financial ends don't meet, we have to work things out. When the door key doesn't seem to fit, we try some very practical problem-solving techniques: first, we jiggle the key; next, we turn it upside down; then, we check to see if we have the right key; finally, if all else fails, we bang on the door to see if someone is inside to let us in.

We are called on to make decisions and solve problems all the time. But very few of us know how to do either very well. Most people reach decisions and solutions by habit and intuition. These methods aren't bad. As we have learned in an earlier chapter, our subconscious thoughts can be stimulated and harnessed somewhat so we can take better advantage of them. In fact, we can even "supercharge" our subconscious mind with raw materials for future decisions and solutions.

For example, Steve's whole graduate education in business administration was by the case-study method. He studied and participated in discussions on about a thousand examples of specific business problems. Part of the reason Harvard uses that approach is to cram a maximum number of simulated experiences into the mind. Since that time Steve has frequently found he has an immediate specific "hunch" on how to attack a problem he is facing. He suspects this is partly due to his extensive case-study experience.

If we have previous experience with a certain kind of situation, our subconscious minds may generate a good decision or solution. It certainly saves time and effort if that happens.

For example, a manager was given an efficiency improvement proposal. The figures showed a possible savings due to the improvement. Intuitively, he sensed that a major cost had been omitted, because it was indirect and hard to quantify. The manager asked the proposers to look specifically at that cost. When they did, they discovered the "improvement" would actually cause the organization to lose money.

At times intuitive feelings are sufficient. But if the situation is complex, the matters are important, and the people involved have different feelings on what should be done, you must be a little more systematic in your problem solving and decision making. Often even problems and decisions which seem simple will benefit greatly from some good, sound thinking on the subject. That is why we are giving you the process presented in this chapter.

It is especially easy to become confused when we are under pressure, and sometimes this is humorous. The following explanations of traffic accidents, actually submitted on insurance forms, were published in the *Toronto Sunday*, July 26, 1977:

"Coming home, I drove into the wrong house, and collided with a tree I don't have!"

"The other car collided with mine without giving warning of his intentions."

"The guy was all over the road. I had to swerve a number of times before I hit him."

"I pulled away from the side of the road, glanced at my mother-in-law and headed over the embankment."[1]

Making decisions and solving problems are often difficult actions for us. We fear making a mistake. According to Lewis Timberlake, 40 percent of our worries are over old decisions.[2]

Clearly there is a need to learn how to solve problems and make decisions. We need to be able to look at situations squarely and confidently, analyze them, and handle them.

In the Scriptures, for example, we find situations where people were exhorted to make decisions: "And if it is disagreeable in your sight to serve the Lord, choose for yourselves today whom you will serve; whether the gods which your father served which were beyond the River, or the gods of the Amorites in whose land you are living; but as for me and my house we will serve the Lord" (Joshua 24:15). "And Elijah came near to all the people and said, 'How long will you hesitate between two opinions? If the Lord is God, follow Him; but if Baal, follow him' " (1 Kings 18:21).

So we need to solve problems and make decisions. The question is how to do both well.

How to Solve Problems and Make Decisions

The following seven steps will help you solve problems and make decisions:

1. Pray.
2. Identify.
3. Establish.
4. Generate.
5. Select.
6. Test.
7. Implement.

Each of these needs some definition and explanation, but if you come to understand and use them, you will be taking a long forward step in making the most of your mind.

1. PRAY.

As in the planning and other ways we use our minds, it is good to gain wisdom from God. In decision making and problem solving, God often places thoughts in our minds as we go. "But he who is spiritual appraises all things. . .but we have the mind of Christ" (1 Corinthians 2:15, 16). As we walk with Him, we qualify as "spiritual" according to this verse and are promised powerful insights on the matter we face.

If for some reason we do not yet see what to do, we only need to ask (Matthew 7:7; James 1:5). When a child yells, "Dad, help!" the father drops what he is doing and goes to help. How much more will God do for us when we say, "Father, help!" Jehoshaphat learned this. When he was in trouble he prayed, "O our God. . .we are powerless. . .nor do we know what to do, but our eyes are on Thee" (2 Chronicles 20:12).

"What makes decision making and problem solving challenging for me," says Steve, "is not usually any single decision or problem, but rather the press of many of them. I don't always have time to be systematic when I am asked to decide on several matters in an hour." As a result, it is even more important that Steve should trust God for wisdom. As mentioned before, he opens and closes each meeting with prayer and sometimes he pauses for prayer in the middle. When he is on the phone considering a hard question, he will often pray silently and sometimes with the other person, "God, what do I do now?"

There are so many human factors and other ramifications involved in decision making, it becomes very hard to know for certain what the right action should be. So it is foolish not to ask the Source of all wisdom to give guidance to us, as He promised He would do.

Make it your habit to pray often and specifically as you consider decisions and problems.

2. IDENTIFY.

Identify the actual problem or decision you face. This sounds easy, but may well be the hardest part of the process.

Consider, for example, the "problem" of heart attacks. Many people are dying at a young age because of them. After much study, the preliminary conclusion has been that too much cholesterol and certain other substances in the blood "cause" this problem by clogging the blood vessels which supply the heart.

That's great to know, but by itself it isn't enough to generate a solution. Further research showed that certain foods, such as butter and eggs, supply cholesterol to the blood stream. The trial solution was to cut back on these types of foods. It was then discovered that this helped a little, but didn't eliminate the problem.

Further research indicated that a big—if not a greater—factor was internal stress. Apparently stress affects the body's chemical balance in such a way that a higher cholesterol level occurs in the blood stream. At last a solution was possible; reduce exposure to stressful situations.

Unfortunately, that also didn't totally solve the problem. Why? Because human beings have a tremendous capability to generate internal stress (worry) even when there is only moderate cause for it. This brings us up to the current "solution" that is being added to the others: learning to relax and drain anxiety from the mind and body.

From the history of "solutions" in this area, it could be that even yet we have not found the true problem—the real cause of heart attacks.

This illustrates the point that it is more difficult to solve a problem when you don't know its cause. Finding the true cause is a little like peeling an artichoke: when you peel back one leaf you find another behind it.

The best and simplest approach we have found is to consider every statement of the "problem" as really only a statement of a "symptom." Keep looking for the cause(s) of this symptom and subsequent ones until you can't seem to find any deeper, underlying cause. When you get to this point, you are probably down to the true problem/cause. Now you can start looking for specific ways to over-come that problem. Doctors do this all the time when they diagnose illnesses. They know there is no point in only putting a bandage on what could be a cancer.

Concerning decisions, you also need to determine the true decision you face. Often we try to "decide," when we really need to "solve" first. Then we can consider alternative solutions. Often we try to make one decision when really a series of decisions is called for and would be much easier to handle. Do you know how to eat an elephant? One bite at a time. So it is with a complete decision situation. Sort through it, one decision at a time.

Suppose, for example, that a person felt the need to buy a new car and now is trying to determine which kind. Let's back up a lit-tle. Is there a problem here? Yes, he has found that it is very im-practical, time-wasting, and nerve-wracking to share his family's one car with his wife. Without going into great detail, no doubt the family has legitimate transportation needs which cannot be met easily with one car. But to leap from there to determining which new car to buy may have bypassed some preliminary decisions. The first deci-sion should be to consider whether to obtain another car at all. There are alternatives: walking, taking the bus or train, riding a bicy-cle or a motor bike, coordinating more carefully, deciding not to go out as often, or occasionally borrowing or renting a car. Many people have lived without two cars, and sometimes without even one car.

Well, suppose our man is able to work through that decision and still concludes that an additional car is best. Now he faces an in-credible number of choices. There are thousands of cars for sale all within a reasonable distance from where he lives. Which lot should he visit? There are various ways to make this decision easier, and one is to divide the decisions into parts. In light of cost, reliability and other considerations, for example, he should be able to deter-mine if he wants a new car or a used car. Now, even if he decides to obtain a new car, he still has to decide whether to buy it or lease it. Ultimately, he may reach his original assumption: he needs to *buy a new car*.

It is very easy to come to the wrong conclusion if you do not consider the right issues. Making decisions involves analyzing future courses of action whenever a choice is possible. Problems usually involve past and current circumstances which are different from what we would like, and as we find the cause of the problem, we must then determine which alternative solution is best.

3. ESTABLISH.

Establish the objectives (criteria) against which your alternatives are measured. What conditions must be met in order for the problem to be solved? What are the factors to consider in making the decision?

This is where you begin to break through the emotional fog that often obscures a decision or a problem. When your child comes crying to you, the first thing you need to find out is what is the matter or what is needed. Until you can calm the child and get some information, it is hard to help him.

Let's go back to our friend who has decided to buy a new car. One of the ways for him to make his decision is to walk down to a car lot without any thought and just buy the first car that appeals to him. He may come home to find he didn't really meet his exact needs and wants. He certainly did want a car that was attractive to him and his family. What else? Well, he probably wanted a certain amount of room.

Suppose he has two small children. He would have needed extra luggage-carrying capacity. The price of the car and projected fuel costs should have been important. Also, reliability (tendency not to break down) is a factor, especially with the possibility of his wife driving the car with the two small children along. Let us assume those are his only five objectives: attractiveness, room, price, fuel economy and reliability.

As stated, each of these is still a little vague. Although our car buyer sort of knows what he means by each of these, it would help him make a good decision later if he could be a little more precise. "Attractiveness" means both he and his wife like the car and feel comfortable being seen in it and having their friends in it. "Room" for him means that he has leg and head room. "Room" for his family means that the car can seat four people comfortably and can carry the play pens, toys and luggage required for a family trip (assuming the other car doesn't already meet this need). "Price" for him means under $8,000, if possible, and no more than $10,000 under any circumstances. (Some people might think more in terms of monthly payments after financing as opposed to total purchase price.) "Fuel economy" for him means 20 or more miles to the gallon. "Reliability" for him means an average or better repair rating in *Consumer Reports*.

In establishing objectives in decisions, there's a need to establish objective priorities in some way. These are rarely equally important to you. It is best to determine which of the objectives are "musts" and which are "wants." Any alternative which does not fulfill a "must" may be eliminated. Another way to prioritize is by "weighing" or giving a value to the objective. One objective may be two or three times as important as the others and an alternative which satisfies that objective has a stronger likelihood of being selected. Another method is simply to run the objectives by the simple priority order of 1, 2, 3, 4, 5. By this, you are saying that it is clearly more important to satisfy the #1 objective than the #5 objective.

Back to our car-buying friend; let's suppose that room and price are "musts" to him and the rest are "wants." From the point of view of "weighing" he would count those two to be twice as important as each of the others. From the point of view of "priority," the five factors would run in this order: (1) room; (2) price; (3) reliability; (4) fuel economy; and (5) appearance. (Normally you won't rank by all three systems on any one decision or problem, but for the sake of a thorough example, we have done so.)

Remember, it is important to establish objectives for a decision or problem. They help you sort out the best alternative from the others. The objectives are often closely related to your personal and job objectives, and they need to be as specific as possible and set up according to priorities.

4. GENERATE.

Generate alternative choices or solutions to your decision or problem. What different ways are possible? What different courses of action seem open to you? How might at least some, if not all, of the objectives be accomplished?

Here is the place to let your mind soar. Go back to the chapter on creativity and apply some of those concepts. To broaden your input, involve other people if that is possible and appropriate. Sometimes it is very important for people to feel a part of a decision, especially if it involves their interest. Brainstorm, but don't criticize any alternatives at first. Take a step back and extend on the normal boundaries of your thinking on this matter. Be open. Sometimes we pass by the best alternative because of our biased perspective. For example, the story is told of a truck driver who drove his vehicle under a low-clearance train trestle. The top of his truck trailer scraped against the lower edge of the trestle and, finally, the truck became stuck. Emergency crews unsuccessfully tried to figure out how to free the truck. Some favored cutting in the trestle. Others favored cutting into the trailer. Finally a little boy came along and offered the best suggestion—"Let the air out of the tires." It worked. Everyone else had limited focus to the area where the trailer was wedged against the trestle. The little boy looked at things from a different perspective—where the trailer was wedged against the road. He did not lack for an alternative.

Many times, though, we face situations where one or two alternatives we see do not look acceptable. For example, Steve was teaching this subject some years ago to a group of Christian workers who were about ready to go to their placement overseas. One young lady was very concerned about the fact that she had put the total responsibility to type, print, and mail her monthly newsletter in the hands of some friends in her home church. As she thought about it, the woman realized she had delegated too much authority. She now wanted to approve the typed content and layout before they were sent out. Unfortunately, she felt they would be offended if she expressed a lack of confidence in them.

She saw two alternatives:

1. Say nothing and have lower quality newsletters.
2. Say something and offend her friends.

But as the group sought to generate additional alternatives for her, a much better alternative arose. The young lady would have a trainer to whom she would be assigned overseas. It would not be unusual for that trainer to want to look over her newsletters before they were sent. She felt it would be much less offensive to approach her friends on the need for her trainer to check over the newsletter. In the process, of course, she would see it too. A little deeper thought generated a satisfactory result.

5. SELECT.

Select the best alternative in light of your objectives. Make a decision. Evaluate the facts of the situation and come to a conclusion.

In the car-buying example, our friend needs to do a preliminary elimination of many alternatives in order to come down to a few which he can consider more carefully. If a car clearly does not satisfy his 'must' objectives, then it can be eliminated immediately. Also, many of his alternatives are really just minor variations from one another. For example, a car of one make and model has many options available. Unless the options relate to the objective, they could serve to complicate the decision. In his case, our car shopper decided to determine which basic type of new car he would buy. Afterwards, he would determine which exact options he would order.

As you evaluate your alternatives against your objectives, it is usually helpful to do a chart (matrix). We'll show you two possible charts. The first looks like this:

OBJECTIVES				ALTERNATIVES		
Weigh-ing	Must/ Want	Priority Order		C	M	F
2X	M	1	Room Head/leg 4 people Extra luggage	Tight	Adequate	Adequate
2X	M	2	Price "Must" no more than $10,000 "Want" less than $8,000	$7,000	$10,000	$7,000
1X	W	3	Reliability Average or better in *Consumer Reports*	Average	Above Average	Average
1X	W	4	Fuel Economy 20 mpg	23	20 – 21	22 – 23
1X	W	5	Appearance To both husband and wife	Better	Acceptable	Acceptable

The letters "C," "M" and "F" stand for specific types of cars he is still considering. The specific facts about each alternative are written in the chart. In some cases, these are estimates and judgments. The ratings to the left of each objective relate to the establishing of priorities he did as explained earlier.

Now, let's help our friends decide. Let's use the "must/want" thinking first.

"F" is the one that satisfies both "musts" well. Furthermore, "F" does acceptably satisfy all the wants.

Turning to the "priority rating" way of thinking, we come to the same conclusion. "F" is better than "C" in the number 1 priority objective and is signifcantly worse than "C" only in the number 5 priority objective. "F" is better than "M" in the number 2 and 4 objectives and is worse in the number 3 objective.

From the point of view of "weighing," the reasoning becomes even clearer. Being better in objectives 1 and 2 is worth two times as much as being better in 3, 4, and 5.

Some of you might be thinking that it is a little unnecessary and overly precise for you to fill out such a complicated chart. So, let's look at the second or simplifed chart:

OBJECTIVES	ALTERNATIVES		
	C	M	F
Room	–	+	+
Price	+	o	+
Reliability	o	+	o
Fuel Economy	+	o	+
Appearance	+	o	o

The main difference between this and the other chart is that it puts less of the thought process on paper. However, it does keep the essence. The mark " + " means that the facts on that alternative more than satisfy the objectives. But " – " means that the alternative really doesn't satisfy the objective. Use "o" as in between – the alternative marginally satisfies the objective. As an example, take the price objective. "C" and "F" more than satisfy even the "less than $8,000" "want" objective. "M" just barely satisies the "no more than $10,000" "must" objective.

One advantage of this refinement is that it is simpler and easier to use. Steve uses it frequently in weighing alternatives against objectives. It takes only a few minutes. It forces him to think the decision or problem through to the point of objectives and alternatives. He can take advantage of any intuition that comes to mind on the subject, harness and focus it toward a firm conclusion. What this approach gives away in precision seems to be more than made up for in usefulness.

It also offers a unique advantage to people who are quantitatively inclined. If you use the "weighing" method of establishing priorities, you can add up the score of each alternative. For example, the "C" alternative figures are $-2 +2 +0 +1 +1$, which give the final score of $+2$ (the algebraic sum of the weighed ratings). The scores of "M" and "F" are $+3$ and $+5$ respectively. Once again, "F" is the best alternative.

Before leaving this "select" point, we would like to add a few thoughts. The two most common errors at this stage are (1) being indecisive and (2) jumping over the process you have started. Concerning indecisiveness, one of the "diseases" of some people is "analysis paralysis." Some people are afraid to, or otherwise don't like to, make a decision so they don't. Joe, the man mentioned at the beginning of this chapter, is an example of this when he tries to order at a restaurant. If a person has this indecision problem, he needs to learn from James 1:6-8 which says, "But let him ask in faith without any doubting, for the one who doubts is like the surf of the sea driven and tossed by the wind. For let not that man expect that he will receive anything from the Lord, being a double-minded man, unstable in all his ways."

Many times either of the two best alternatives will do an adequate job. The time and mental anguish for yourself and others may exceed the cost of choosing a mildly "wrong" alternative. If you have gone through the above process, the worst you will normally select is the less good of two acceptable choices. If your decision proves "wrong," normally you will make a new decision and learn from the experience. Obviously, we are not advocating carelessness, especially in decisions in which the matters are important and there is no opportunity to decide again. But for most of us, those cases are few. Some people have the opposite problem from indecisiveness. They are often wrong, but seldom in doubt. By the time they get to the select step, they have just about had it with all this analysis. They want to get on with it. But they need to learn from Proverbs 24:2-3 which says, "For their minds devise violence, and their lips talk of trouble. By wisdom a house is built, and by understanding it is established."

6. TEST.

Test your selected alternative for flaws which may not have surfaced earlier in your thinking. Normally, you can compensate for these flaws as you implement. Occasionally you will want to change your choice at this point.

One very serious potential flaw is that we just don't want to bear the risk of some undesirable outcome. Many people are overly risk averse. But all of us have some aversion to it. If, for example, our whole financial nest egg is to be invested in something, we want it to be a fairly sure thing. Some alternative investments may show a higher expected return but have too much risk of total.

In our car buying example, there are some risks to consider. Has the objective of reliability been adequately weighed in light of the potential consequences of his wife and children being stranded on the road? The man may conclude that it has since they would almost always be traveling during the day and not too far from home.

There is normally at least one person in any group who can shoot holes in every plan. If that happens to you, take heart. When Jesus announced He was going up to Jerusalem to be killed as a part of God's overall plan, He received quite a bit of resistance from the disciples.

Another key test is whether there is an indication of a lack of God's blessing on an alternative. This is especially true in bigger, more important decisions. Normally we can expect a confirming sense of peace about the right alternative. It is a subtle way for God to verify His blessing. As we operate with the "mind of Christ," we can assume that God has been the ultimate author of our thoughts. If for some reason our heads haven't been listening properly, God works on our hearts.

Some years ago, Steve was offered a job that absolutely was his life's dream. It perfectly fit his training and personality. Yet, as he prayed and thought about taking the job, Steve had great turmoil in his heart. Clearly, God was saying, "No!"

Another test is the "human factor" test. An alternative may look good on paper, but people aren't ready to buy it yet. For example, some years ago the president of a particular organization tried to propose a name change. It made sense from a rational point of view. The problem was that a major portion of the organization would have been deeply offended. So, he didn't do it.

Another test is timing. Is it best to implement this alternative now, in three weeks, or in one year? If later, then what, if anything, needs to be done now?

Even after all these facts, most initial choices still stand as the best alternatives. Usually the testing confirms and consolidates the decision. For example, Judy and Steve carefully prayed and thought through whether they would have children. They came up with eleven very good reasons to do so. But there were seven significant negative considerations. They had basically decided "Yes," but took the trouble to address each "negative consideration" and seek to compensate for it. For example, children would probably severely curtail Judy's career as a magazine editor. Yet, she and Steve determined that her skills in writing and editing could continue to be used on a less formal basis. As the birth of their first child neared, Judy retired from her position as editor of the *Worldwide Challenge* magazine. However, since then she has finished a book and has written several articles. And since their second child's birth, she has continued, at a slower pace, on her writing projects.

7. IMPLEMENT.

It doesn't do any good to make a decision if no action follows. Implement the finally selected alternative. Put it into action. Don't assume this happens automatically after a decision or solution is determined.

Harry Truman made this comment when General Eisenhower was elected President of the United States: "Poor Ike. When he was a general, he gave an order and it was carried out. Now he is going to sit in that big office and he will give an order and ain't nothing going to happen."

What are some ways to implement? First, complete the plan. You learned about planning in a previous chapter. You already have prayed, established objectives and started to implement a program. What additional specific steps are needed to move forward? What is the appropriate schedule? For example: When should you start? When should you be done? What, if any, budget is needed and from where will it come?

In our earlier example, our friend needed to order or pick out his car. He may have needed to arrange financing. He certainly needed to increase his insurance policy. After all these matters were attended to, he was able to drive his new car off the lot.

Next, make sure someone has accepted the responsibility for implementation. Of course, that may be you. Is someone committed? One of the familiar statements you may hear in monthly committee meetings is, "What did we ever do about last month's decision to. . .?" Probably it was never assigned to a specific member of the committee to implement.

If other people are involved in implementation, is it reasonable to assume that they already see the need and are motivated to pursue this course of action? If not, what can be done to provide some motivation?

Look back in your own experience. How many significant projects have been completed without some follow-up effort? Not too many. So how are you going to follow-up the implementation of your decision or solution? Are you going to put a note on your calendar, arrange a meeting or what?

Be sure to pray (and ask others to pray) for the successful implementation of your decision or solution.

Finally, begin! Learn from the Lord's admonition to Moses just before the children of Israel crossed the Red Sea, "Why are you crying out to Me? Tell the sons of Israel to go forward" (Exodus 14:15).

SUMMARY

In summary, to solve a problem or make a decision you need to:
1. Pray.
2. Identify.
3. Establish.
4. Generate.
5. Select.
6. Test.
7. Implement.

The first letters of these words form the acrostic, "piegsti," which sounds like "pigsty." Indeed, our lives can turn out to be a little messy if we don't know how to make decisions and solve problems.

Pause for a moment and determine a decision or problem you currently face. If you can, start applying this process to it, right now.

I. PERSONAL APPLICATION

What is your highest personal priority application point found in the principles presented in this chapter? Enter that point in the indicated place in the Personal Application Worksheet at the end of the book. In the column next to that enter some specific plans to help you start implementing that point.

II. THOUGHT QUESTIONS

1. How good is my intuition in making decisions and solving problems? Are there times when it falls short?
2. Of the seven steps in solving problems and making decisions outlined in this chapter, which two are my weakest points, and how can I improve them?
3. Of the two suggested charts on this subject, which is the more helpful to me in light of how I tend to think and operate?
4. Is there someone I know who makes decisions or solves problems well? How can I learn from this person?

III. ACTION PROJECT

Think of the three hardest problems or decisions you now face. Apply this chapter's approach to them. Involve other people in your thinking, as appropriate.

IV. FURTHER STUDY MATERIALS

For more information on problem solving and decision making, you will want to consider the Further Study Materials for this chapter listed at the end of the book.

13

REMEMBERING AND FORGETTING

"By the way, my name is Jack Sales. What is yours?"

"Sam Evans."

"We are certainly flying over some scenic country today, aren't we?"

"Yes. I always enjoy seeing the Grand Canyon from an airplane."

"Say. . .um. . .er. . .What did you say your name was again?"

"Sam Evans."

Familiar story? Have you ever forgotten a person's name within a minute after hearing it? It was almost as if you hadn't heard it at all, or as if your memory was some sort of revolving door. It lets the name in, spins it around and lets it right back out. Embarrassing, isn't it? It makes you wonder if you are getting prematurely senile.

Well, don't panic. Most people have experienced the same thing.

It is known as selective perception. You literally never focused on the person's name and you immediately became distracted by something else. So, it is common, but is not very desirable.

The purpose of this chapter is to help you train your memory. You will learn some ways to retain knowledge beyond what might seem possible to you. You also will learn to decide what you don't want to retain and to drain that from your conscious mind.

The Scriptures suggest that both remembering and forgetting are important activities. The "forgetting" part may be a revelation to many readers, although we know we're to remember many things, as: "Remember all the commandments of the Lord, so as to do them and not follow after your own heart and your own eyes" (Numbers 15:39). "Remember the words of the Lord Jesus" (Acts 20:35). "And Moses said to the people, 'Remember this day in which you went out from Egypt, from the house of slavery; for by a powerful hand the Lord brought you out from this place'" (Exodus 13:3). "And when He had given thanks, He broke it, and said, 'This is My body, which is for you; do this in remembrance of Me'" (1 Corinthians 11:24). "Wise men store up knowledge" (Proverbs 10:14).

But as much as the Scriptures tell us to remember, there are a surprising number of verses about forgetting. For example, "I will not remember your sins" (Isaiah 43:25b). "God has made me forget all my trouble" (Genesis 41:51). "But one thing I do: forgetting what lies behind and reaching forward to what lies ahead, I press on toward the goal . . ." (Philippians 3:13). "And be kind to one another, tender-hearted, forgiving each other just as God in Christ also has forgiven you" (Ephesians 4:32 — implying we should forgive and forget the sins of others just as God does ours).

It makes sense that we should remember the mandates of the Word of God and should forgive and forget the sins of others against us. Unfortunately, most of us do a lot better at forgetting the Word and remembering people's sins. God wouldn't ask us to do something that we couldn't trust Him for the power to do. So, we ought to be able to discipline our minds to remember and forget correctly.

Developing a trained memory is not a new human endeavor. Greek and Roman orators used to memorize lengthy speeches and deliver them accurately, word for word, without notes. They accomplished this through the technique of association. They, of course, had no trouble recalling the various rooms and furnishings they encountered as they walked through their homes. Therefore, they associated each point of talks with an item in the home, in the sequence in which they would encounter them at home. Each location or place formed a memory hook on which they could hang a concept. That is where we get the phrases "in the first place," "in the second place," and so on.

Your memory can be trained to either remember or forget. First, let's consider that most people quickly see the need to do better, but the question is "How?" What follows gives the answer.

How to Remember

The following are five actions that have proven very helpful in remembering things:

1. Determine.
2. Observe.
3. Associate.
4. "Ridiculize."
5. Substitute.

You will learn more about the meanings of these concepts as you read on. Pause for a moment here, though, and start your new emphasis on remembering. Notice that the first letters of the five words spell "DOARS" which is a misspelling of "DOORS." Form in your mind the image of several doors shaped like A's. Perhaps you could think of them as entrances to an A-frame mountain cabin. The A shape of the doors will remind you that the acrostic DOARS has an A in it.

These concepts will open new doors for you. By remembering the A-shaped doors you will be remembering concepts. We will elaborate more on this illustration at the end of this section. Now, let's dig into "how to remember."

1. DETERMINE.

The first step is to determine whether or not something is worth remembering. The name of someone you are going to see again is generally worth remembering. How far apart two cities are in some other country of the world is generally not worth remembering.

You need to determine how useful it is to you to have the item in your readily accessible memory, as opposed to having it available in some reference book or place. Take telephone numbers as an example. Any number you frequently call is probably worth memorizing. It regularly saves you time. On the other hand, there is certainly no need to memorize every number in the telephone book just because some day you may call some of those numbers. The telephone book is always available to help you find infrequently called numbers.

Most people try to use their memories to handle items that are better handled by other methods. A schedule item is a good example. Some people do not keep a written schedule. When someone makes an appointment with them, they simply make a mental note of it. Hopefully, when the day and hour of the appointment arrives, they will recall it and show up. Unfortunately, we all have been the victims of people who use that system and then forget about their appointments. Unless a person does not have many activities, that method of scheduling can be unreliable.

More serious is the additional liability incurred when memorizing scheduled items clutters the processing function of the mind and causes anxiety. The mind is not able to function at maximum efficiency and effectiveness. If we are worried about forgetting something, we are not one hundred percent focused on what we want to think about. Since there are good alternative ways to "remember" scheduled items (e.g., keeping a calendar/schedule and forming the habit of looking at it several times a day), it is a waste of mental energy to memorize them.

Carefully screen what you commit to memory. Implementing the following steps involves some work and a definite mental focus. Before you start the process ask, "Is it worth it?" and "Are there other ways I can find this information when I need it, beside recalling it from memory?" Use the other ways when you can and let your mind focus on what's important to remember.

2. OBSERVE.

Focus on what you have determined to remember to get a clear image of it in your mind. You cannot recall later what you do not originally observe. Aristotle opened one of his books with the statement, "It is impossible even to think without a mental picture."[1] He goes on to say in De anima, "It is the image-making part of the mind which makes the work of the higher processes of thought possible. Hence the mind never works without a mental picture. The thinking faculty thinks of its form in pictures. No one could ever learn or understand anything if he had not the faculty of perception."[2]

One illustration of this principle is the use of logos in advertising companies and products. Do you remember the label picturing a girl walking through the rain with an umbrella over her head and a carton of salt under her arm, spilling salt as she walked? That is the logo of Morton Salt. It immediately calls to mind the words, "When it rains, it pours." Through the use of a clear, understandable picture, for years the Morton Salt Company has enabled us to recall one of the distinctive features of its product.

When you see or hear of the rock of Gibraltar, you probably think of the Prudential Life Insurance Company. When you see two golden arches along the road, you think of McDonald's. If it is anywhere near mealtime and you like McDonald's food, you many even feel a hunger pang.

One of the keys to observing carefully is being motivated to do so. For example, it would be unusual for the ordinary person to want to memorize the location or position of hundreds of the stars in the sky. If a person is a navigator, he has good reason to want to memorize the positions and configurations of the stars—they help him know where he is.

If you have determined something is worth memorizing because it has value to you, that will provide the needed motivation.

Another key to observing is concentration. At the beginning of this chapter you read an illustration of a person forgetting the name of someone he just met. This occurs because of a lack of focus or concentration on the name. Most of us move on to thinking about our first impression of a person (or what we are going to say to that person) and we don't think long enough about his or her name to remember it.

We can cure this problem by concentrating on the first words someone says to us. If we make the act of learning a person's name a priority item, we simultaneously are making it important enough to concentrate on and remember.

3. ASSOCIATE.

The key to being able to recall things is association. Links between mental images enable us to call up a whole string of concepts which are related to some initial mental image. For example, when you see someone whom you haven't seen for years, you immediately think of activities you shared years ago with that person. You probably had not thought of those activities for a long time. But links in your mind between that person and those activities now flood your consciousness with memories.

Professor Robert E. Brennen declares in his book, *General Psychology*, "Any part of an experience which we had at a previous time has a tendency to recall other parts of the same experience whenever the first part comes into our consciousness."

Another way to associate is by connection to an easily remembered event. For example, Steve remembers that he was in a laboratory at school when he heard that President Kennedy had been shot, even though that was many years ago. Lee was running an electric train as a young department store clerk when President Roosevelt announced our nation was at war with Japan. Many Americans can remember what they were doing when President Nixon resigned and when President Reagan was shot.

Harry Lorayne and Jerry Lucas make the flat statement in their best seller, *The Memory Book*, "All memory, whether trained or untrained is based on association."[3]

There are many other ways to associate items, including by category, specific action together with or as parts of a whole. The value of association in remembering is that when you can link several items together in a "memory chain," you can recall all of the items if any one of them comes to your attention. All that is left, then, is for one of the items to come to your attention.

For example, suppose you want to memorize several Bible verses and illustrations related to each of the top ten areas of need you encounter in people's lives. You can do this by forming ten different chains, one for each area of need. At the beginning of each chain should be a mental picture related to a person having that particular need. That picture then will link easily with the cirumstances in which you are counseling a person with the need. Once you have the first item on a particular chain, all of the rest of the items will be remembered, i.e., the appropriate Bible verses and illustrations.

Three other concepts will probably prove helpful to you as you seek to form strong association links: repetition, substitution, ridiculousness. We will cover the last two as separate points which follow. Briefly, though, let us cover repetition here.

We have often heard, "Repetition aids learning." The apostle Peter said, "I shall always be ready to remind you of these things" (2 Peter 1:12). As we repeat actions, we form habits. Likewise, as we repeat thoughts, we form memories which are easier to recall. In trying to remember a person's name, for example, one good thing you can do is to repeat the name several times in your mind. Use the name in your conversation while you are determining how to associate it with the person.

4. "RIDICULIZE."

This is a coined word to make a point stronger. Suppose you were going to the store and wanted to remember to buy a loaf of bread, a can of motor oil and a bag of oranges. They are probably not located anywhere near one another in the store and they aren't very similar. How can you remember without a written list? Imagine the following association: Picture a loaf of bread floating on a sea of motor oil and a man in a nearby rowboat throwing oranges at floating oil cans. Ridiculous? Yes. Therefore, you will remember it better and longer.

Our minds are flooded with information, most of which is fairly routine. We have become quite proficient at keeping most of this information from being easily remembered. However, when something unusual comes along, we tend to stop, focus, and think about it. This greatly increases its chances of being easily remembered.

In *De anima* Aristotle said, "The perceptions brought in by the five senses are first treated or worked upon by the faculty of imagination, and it is the images so formed which become the material of the intellectual faculty. Imagination is the intermediary between perception and thought."[4]

There are several ways to make our mental images ridiculous. One is to distort the size and shape of the item. Suppose, for example, you are trying to associate the last name "Debose" with the face of a person you just met. If the person has a pretty large nose, a natural distortion would be to picture the person's nose as very over-sized, perhaps red and stopped up due to a cold. Under this huge overhang picture a sign which says, "The Nose." The nose, sounding like Debose, helps you remember the name.

Another method is to increase the numbers or quantity involved. If in your memory chain you want to remember to buy a carton of milk you may want to picture hundreds of thousands of half-gallon milk cartons.

Another method is to create action in the memory chain. If in the milk carton example you wanted to remember to buy distilled water, you could picture the milk cartons going over a huge, thunderous waterfall, such as Niagara Falls.

5. SUBSTITUTE.

Some items you want to memorize are fairly intangible when it comes to forming a graphic mental picture. In these cases, it is helpful to substitute more tangible pictures to form your associations. These pictures must, of course, be traceable back to the original item.

One of the most common needs for substitution is with numbers. In his book, *Stop Forgetting*, Dr. Bruno Furst outlines one good way to make numbers more tangible. Each number is associated with a consonant sound:[5]

1	2	3	4	5	6	7	8	9	0
t	n	m	r	l	j	k	f	p	z

Any series of numbers can then be converted to one or more words by simply supplying vowel sounds in between. For example, the number 78 would have the consonant sounds "k" and "f" in that order. The words "cough", "cuff", or "coffee" would have these consonant sounds with only vowel sounds added.

Each of those is a good deal more tangible and available for "ridiculizing" and associating than is the number 78. For example, if you wanted to remember that a friend of yours lives at 78 Hawthorne, picture him drinking hundreds of cups of coffee in front of his house until he starts to laugh ("ha") uncontrollably and finally sits down on the rose bushes and jumps back up because he sat on a thorn.

Now you are left with only the problem of associating the consonant sounds with numbers, which is a fairly limited memorization.

Another common need for subsitution is with people's names. It is generally easy to substitute a sound-alike tangible concept for the name. For example, Douglass can be pictured as a very small hole having just been dug with a totally exhausted person sitting next to it while a much bigger hole is in progress right next to it. Roddy can be pictured as a long iron rod bent into the shape of a "d." Lee sometimes tells people, "My surname rhymes easily with 'body,' or 'toddy'!"

Summary of How to Remember

In summary of this first part of the chapter, there are five basic actions that will help you commit something to memory: determine, observe, associate, "ridiculize", and substitute. As you apply these actions you will need to focus your attention and unleash your imagination. There are many more specific ways these concepts can apply to memorizing the contents of a book, musical notes, or even a talk outline.

If you have a special interest in reading more about this, you will find a number of books and articles available in the library or bookstore. One of the best, most widely available books we have found is *The Memory Book*. Also see the further study materials section at the end of this book.

To give you one last example and to help you remember the five key remembering concepts, see if you can picture the following memory assocation chain.

Remember the A shaped doors from earlier in this chapter? Picture one of them at the entrance to an old mine whose support timbers are teetering constantly. (Teetering mine = determine) Right at the entrance to the mine are hundreds of telescopes focused on a scene way down the horizontal mine shaft. (Hundreds of

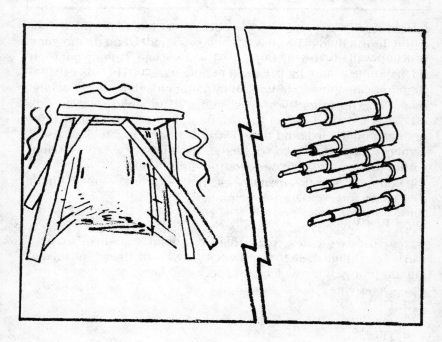

telescopes = observe) The scene at the other end of the mine shaft is very unusual. In plain view is a huge sock tacked up on the mine wall in the shape of a "T." (A sock a T = associate) Peering out from the toes of this huge sock is a pair of bulging eyes. These eyes seem to be reading a message written in the liquid, slimey "ick" on the mine floor. (Read ick eyes = "ridiculize") Suddenly, the eyes look off to the side and see what must be a fleet of small submarines sailing through the liquid slime with a stick attached to each rising up above the slime. On top of each stick is a factory whistle "tooting" with a loud noise. (Sub stick toot = substitute)

If you mull over this memory chain a few times, you will find it difficult to forget how to remember.

How to Forget

Now that we see how to discipline our minds to remember, how can we discipline them to forget what we want to forget? The following are four actions which will specifically help you forget:

1. Determine.
2. Drain.
3. Displace.
4. Disdain.

You can see that they all start with "D" and if you practice these, you could nearly flunk any memory test.

1. DETERMINE.

Determine whether or not you want to forget particular things. If you know ahead of time that you do, you can arrange it so that they never seriously enter your memory.

A certain executive has exceptionally busy days. Sometime he will have 8-10 meetings daily on totally different subjects. If he carries over his thoughts from earlier meetings into his later ones, he can't be of much use. If he is worried about whether or not he will remember to take action on every point from each meeting, he will be a mental wreck by evening. So, during the day, he has to clear the "debris" from his mind on a regular basis.

You will learn more about how to do this in subsequent points, but let's pause here to draw a contrast. Another executive we know is the sort of man who can't seem to forget. He has trouble, sometimes, focusing on his current meeting because he is still emotionally and mentally involved in the previous one. He can't go to sleep easily because his mind stays in high gear, reviewing the events of the day and second-guessing his decisions and actions. It is not surprising that he is often mentally exhausted, up tight and sleepy. He even suffers from some of the physical ailments that stem from anxiety.

Learning to forget is not a total cure for anxiety, but it is a good start. Many things don't need to be remembered, and if we don't remember them, it is difficult to worry about them.

2. DRAIN

Learn to count on other systems besides your mind to accomplish certain things and "drain" your concerns into these systems. Earlier in the chapter, we mentioned the value of keeping a calendar or schedule. If you have formed the habit of consulting your schedule regularly and faithfully, entering all of your time commitments in it, you will have no further need to remember appointments.

However, be sure you have your habits operating well before you stop remembering. Years ago Steve and his roommate were scheduled to eat dinner at some friends' house on a particular day. Steve had only done project work on that day, so he didn't even consult his pocket schedule, knowing he had no appointments during the day. When evening came, he and his roommate had totally forgotten their dinner engagement. They ate at a cafeteria and really gorged themselves—including apple pie a la mode. When they returned to their house, Steve was sleepy and decided to take a nap. As he took off his slacks, his pocket calendar fell out and opened to the day's date. He looked down in horror, noticing the dinner engagement. He and his roommate still had time to get there, so they rushed over and never let on that they had eaten. Their hosts fixed an enormous meal. "By the time I left their house," Steve recalls, "my roommate almost had to roll me to the car."

A word to the wise on scheduling and any other system: work at it diligently.

There are some other simple systems that can further relieve your memory. For example, when one person we know is about to leave on a trip, he starts a few days before by beginning a checklist of items to take which he might forget. Normal things, such as shaving kit and clothes don't need any special effort to remember. But it does require effort to remember a typed speech, work files, or items to deliver. He can wake up in the middle of the night wondering if he will remember—unless he either writes it down or stacks it visibly in a corner in his office.

Regarding meetings and other sources of items for him to do, this person has one stack in his office for things he personally handles and another for things he is going to delegate to his secretary and others later. He tosses action items into one of those two stacks and totally forgets about them as he goes to his next meeting.

Another refinement that is particularly useful in an office setting is a follow-up system. For example, a secretary can purchase a special accordion file with one slot for each day of the month, as well as some slots for future months. She then can check daily to see if any correspondence has been placed in the slot for follow-up purposes on that day.

One little system you can use at home is to stack in one place things that are going to the office in the morning.

Another helpful idea is to keep a note pad handy at all times to jot down ideas that need action or further thought. This is especially helpful at night and during prayer times. If creative thinking wakes you up in the middle of the night, turn on your flashlight, write down your thoughts and go back to sleep without any fear of forgetting by morning. If you are distracted in your prayer time by something you need to do later, write it down and then turn your thoughts back to God.

3. `DISPLACE.

One of the best methods for removing a thought from your consciousness is to displace it with another thought. God tells us to use this technique to displace inappropriate thoughts about this world. In Colossians 3:1-2, we read, "If then you have been raised up with Christ, keep seeking the things above, where Christ is, seated at the right hand of God. Set your mind on the things above, not on the things that are on earth." As we focus on God and the things of heaven, we are not focusing on earth and its concerns.

Exactly how can you make displacement a way of life? When Steve wants to make progress at writing a book, he has to get away from the office and from the center of activities of his home. He either goes out of town or retreats to his study room at home and shuts the door. He starts by immediately focusing on the outline, the research, and the other materials which relate to the book. In less than an hour he is in another world. His mind is totally focused on the book.

He can also focus on a project during an airplane trip and have similar results. He really gets into it. He hardly notices other conversations and noises.

Lee learned to displace all sounds of a newspaper's city room when writing stories for the next edition. He could do this so well that often someone would stand beside him without his being aware of that person until he was spoken to.

In studying the Scriptures and praying, sometimes it is helpful to read or pray aloud to further displace other distractions. It sometimes helps to listen to the Scriptures or praise music on tapes in the car as you are driving. This audibly displaces other thoughts that can distract you.

One man we know likes to jog, and if something is particularly distracting, he will go out and run harder than normal. This requires so much physical and mental focus, it drives other thoughts from his mind.

Sometimes, it is good to talk to someone on another subject and really get deeply engrossed in the conversation.

When something is distracting you and you want to forget it, thinking about something else will displace the original thought. For more on displacing, review the chapter on anxiety.

4. DISDAIN

You will never have to worry about forgetting if you do not memorize in the first place. That saves a lot of extra effort trying to remove things later.

One way of doing this is to make sure you don't do any of the key steps toward memorizing when something unworthy comes to your attention. Immediately determine that it isn't worth remembering. Don't focus on it or observe it carefully. Don't associate. Don't "ridiculize," and don't substitute. If you discard and ignore a thought quickly enough, you may be able to prevent if from lodging firmly in your conscious memory.

A better way, of course, is never to *encounter* the observation. We know a man who is a sports fan. Sometimes his favorite teams do well, and sometimes they don't. Sometimes he and his wife will listen to a baseball game on the radio while they are doing other things. If their team is playing poorly, it can actually discourage the husband a little. When that begins to happen, he turns off the radio or leaves the room. He doesn't want his mind to absorb and remember what he is hearing.

One of the best methods of "disdaining" is delegation of a whole area of activity. When others are handling whole areas of activity, you are much less involved, and therefore, have fewer occasions to have to forget problems or other worries. If this option is open to you, and if qualified people can and should take some of your responsibilities, this can be an excellent help.

Summary of How to Forget

Remember, here's how you forget: determine, drain, displace, disdain. To help you remember this, consider the following memory chain association: Picture a man scratching his head (can't remember) while looking at a huge road sign where the highway crosses ten sets of railroad tracks. The sign says, "Detour — Mines Ahead." (Detour mines = Determine.) The sign is moving back and forth and has a large arrow pointing toward the train tracks. This man and thousands of other people waiting there leave their cars and hop on several waiting trains. (Train = Drain. Remember, all the words start with "D.") The trains speed off and travel for miles until they encounter millions of signs alongside the tracks saying, "This is the place!" (This place = Displace.) When the trains stop, a great fear fills the thousands of people and they scatter in all directions. (Scatter in all directions = Disdain.)

SUMMARY OF THE CHAPTER

Most people do not remember things well. In addition, most find it difficult to push unwanted, distracting thoughts out of their minds.

Yet, it is possible to train and discipline our minds to remember and to forget. It requires concentration and creativity, but the results can be startling.

Our usual chapter ending includes a review of the principles' points. But for this chapter, we'll let you do it. Can you recall the five key concepts in remembering? Can you recall the four key concepts in forgetting? If not, go back and review the memory chains before leaving this chapter. These are two outlines you should never forget.

— — —

I. PERSONAL APPLICATION

What is your highest personal priority application point found in the principles presented in this chapter? Enter that point in the indicated place in the Personal Application Worksheet at the end of the book. In the column next to that enter some specific plans to help you start implementing that point.

II. THOUGHT QUESTIONS

1. What is it that I have the most trouble remembering? How can I apply what I have learned to that?
2. How can I apply these memory principles to Bible memory? Can I memorize a verse a day for the next week?
3. In Philippians 3:13 Paul says, "Forgetting what lies behind and

reaching forward to what lies ahead, I press on toward the goal."
How can I apply that principle better to my life?
4. What time management, follow-up and other systems can I
   use to take a memory load off my mind?

III. ACTION PROJECT

Just for fun and practice, see if you can memorize the
name of everyone you meet in the next social affair you
attend.

IV. FURTHER STUDY MATERIALS

For more information on remembering and forgetting, you
will want to consider the Further Study Materials for this
chapter listed at the end of the book.

14

SPEAKING AND WRITING

Someone recently said to a person who does public speaking, "I look forward to hearing you speak. You always have something worthwhile to say. Your illustrations are classic and they really communicate. I find your lessons interesting and helpful to me."

This statement was made to a person who was formerly an uninteresting communicator. But over a period of years, he learned to apply some of the lessons we are going to share with you in this chapter.

Up to this point we have talked about how to infuse information into our minds and how to process it there. Now we are going to show you how to send information out.

There are a number of subtle ways of communicating, such as by using gestures and facial expressions, but this chapter will focus on the most common methods: speaking and writing.

In Proverbs 15:2 and 7 we find, "The tongue of the wise makes knowledge acceptable, but the mouth of fools spouts folly. The lips of the wise spread knowledge, but the hearts of fools are not so."

We want to show you how to communicate well.

Our opportunities to communicate vary in length, formality and situation. Sometimes we have an opportunity to take part in a conversation with someone or perhaps to write a short note. Other times the opportunity is to communicate more formally and at greater length. We may be called upon to deliver a talk or to write a report or article. The principles of this chapter are applicable to all forms of communication. In shorter and more informal situations, you will not apply every point before you participate, but you may discover certain areas of weakness which you want to strengthen and you will probably keep them in mind.

Over a period of time, as you focus on different areas, you will see significant improvement in your ability to communicate. When you prepare for a longer, more formal communique, such as a speech or paper, you definitely will want to look through this check list of principles.

Overview

There are three major procedures used in communicating:
A. Be - Be the kind of person people listen to.
B. Plan - Think about what you are going to communicate.
C. Motivate - Cause your audience to be motivated by and
     responsive to your communication.

Let's look at each of the procedures in more detail.

A. Be - Be the Kind of Person People Listen To.

The following are a number of attitudes and actions which contribute to your credibility as a communicator. People will tend to listen more carefully to the person who implements these suggestions:

1. Walk closely with God.
2. Love people.
3. Model your message.
4. Know your strengths and build on them.
5. Be teachable and humble.
6. Have a joyful heart and countenance.
7. Listen and be sensitive to what others are saying and feeling.
8. Speak the truth.

Now, let's examine each subpoint in more detail.

1. WALK CLOSELY WITH GOD

God is the source of all wisdom. He gives us special capability to discern the needs of people at a given time. God literally can give us words to say in any situation. As you walk closely with Him, you will possess supernatural communication skills.

Even if you are nervous, hesitant, or tongue-tied, God can help you become a more effective communicator. Remember the story of Moses? God ordered him to go before Pharoah and speak, but Moses declined because he said he was not an eloquent orator. God then promised to *make* Moses become a gifted spokesman. But Moses lacked faith and confidence. As a result, God withdrew the offer to bless Moses with oratory gifts and, instead, instructed him to take his brother Aaron to act as spokesman. Aaron obeyed. Later, Aaron was made chief priest and religious teacher of the Jews. As you walk with God, you receive special blessings and special abilities.

In addition, you will gain respect from people beyond any you could muster in your own strength. Most people have a very high view of God, and if you seem to be in communication with Him and have a message from Him, most people will be interested in hearing from you. It has been said that when Billy Graham steps into a room, the whole atmosphere changes. He carries with him the aura of the presence of God. When he speaks, people do, indeed, listen.

2. LOVE PEOPLE.

Jesus said, "By this all men will know that you are My disciples, if you have love one for another" (John 13:35).

Clearly, love communicates a message. It is one of the main ways God uses to communicate Himself to men. In 1 John 4:7, 8 we find, "Beloved, let us love another, for love is from God; and everyone who loves is born of God and knows God. The one who does not love does not know God, for God is love."

Love is of paramount importance in our lives. Paul wrote, "If I speak with the tongues of men and of angels, but do not have love, I have become a noisy gong or a clanging cymbal. And if I have the gift of prophesy, and know all mysteries and all knowledge; and if I have all faith, so as to remove mountains, but do not have love, I am nothing. And if I give all my possessions to feed the poor, and if I deliver my body to be burned, but do not have love, it profits me nothing" (1 Corinthians 13:1-3).

Love exerts a great force on people. God uses this force to attract us to Himself. He uses it as the glue to hold people together in relationships. And God can use that same force in your life to help you be a powerful communicator.

Ney Bailey, a national representative of Campus Crusade for Christ, travels widely and speaks to many audiences. Through her speaking and writing, she has a powerful effect on people. She clearly communicates her love and concern and she gives from her heart. That is why, when Ney speaks, people listen.

3. MODEL YOUR MESSAGE.

What do your actions say to people? People are watching you to determine how believable you are. Be sure there is consistency in what you say and what you do. Otherwise, your life may shout so loudly people cannot hear what you say.

A certain minister's children found a stray dog and his whole family quickly became attached to it. They watched for advertisements or other word from someone who lost a dog that looked like this one, but for a long time they saw none. During that time they became even more attached to the animal. Finally, though, a man who had lost his dog made contact with the minister and described his dog in great detail. It matched perfectly.

When the minister told the children the owner was coming for the dog, they were so upset that he decided to take some drastic action. He cut the few very distinctive white hairs off the animal's tail. When the man arrived to claim his dog the dog recognized his owner, but the minister protested that this could not be the man's dog because he did not exactly match the description the man had given. In particular, the minister said, the dog did not have white hairs on his tail. Despite the visitor's objections the minister finally persuaded him that this was not his dog and the man did not take it.

But the family knew the truth. Over the years that incident, plus other inconsistencies in the minister's life, caused his children to shun the Christian faith. None of them now walks closely with God. Why? Because in their eyes, their dad was a phony. His verbal messages could not overcome his life's message.

4. KNOW YOUR STRENGTHS AND BUILD ON THEM.

God has given us strengths. In many cases, we have special knowledge gained from our experience or education. We may have a special sensitivity to certain needs of particular people. God also has given us certain strengths in our method of communicating. We may have a good credibility with people or good logic, humor or personal style.

We should seek to use our strengths as often as possible. If you are particularly good at speaking informally with people, one-to-one, then seek those kinds of settings and make the most of them. When you speak to a larger group, view it as a situation where you are speaking to one individual. Many good speakers are effective because they are personable. They make people feel as though they are talking just to them.

5. BE TEACHABLE AND HUMBLE.

The following is a sampling of important communication lessons from Proverbs 15:5,22, 31-33: "He who regards reproof is prudent. . . . Without consultation, plans are frustrated, but with many counselors they succeed. . . . He whose ear listens to the life-giving reproof will dwell among the wise. . .before honor comes humility."

In Philippians 2:5-7 we see the example of Christ: "Have this attitude in yourselves which was also in Christ Jesus, who, although He existed in the form of God, did not regard equality with God as a thing to be grasped, but emptied Himself, taking the form of a bond-servant and being made in the likeness of men."

6. HAVE A JOYFUL HEART AND COUNTENANCE.

Looks communicate. Many people look stern and forbidding and, therefore, do not communicate as well as they would like. Lee remembers being told when he was in high school some 40 years ago, that he looked mean. "I had deliberately cultivated that look to avoid physical attacks by my peers," says Lee. "Although many surgeries had corrected my physical problems so that none were evident, I was no match for other boys my age. The *mean* look got me entirely through school without a single fight.

"When I became a salesman in my twenties, however, my countenance was often cited as something which worked against me. I then spent many years reversing my severe look. I didn't fully succeed until after I made my Christian commitment."

As a contrast, Steve's former secretary Vicki, apparently learned early in life to be quite joyful. From time to time, Steve would tell her that even if she didn't type and take shorthand well (which she did), he would still want to keep her around just to encourage him. Vicki's joyful countenance made her easy to listen to.

7. LISTEN AND BE SENSITIVE TO WHAT OTHERS ARE SAYING AND FEELING.

When people sense you are a listener, they tend to reciprocate and listen to you. It is very easy to cut people short or appear not to be interested in what they are saying. If that is your habit, it affects your ability to communicate and be listened to. Cultivate the skills you learned earlier in this book on receiving information into your mind. Listen and observe aggressively when others are speaking. You'll learn a lot, but you'll also build credibility. You'll be prepared to relate to people.

8. SPEAK THE TRUTH.

When you do say something, make sure it is the truth as nearly as you are able to determine. Ephesians 4:25 says, "Therefore, laying aside falsehood, speak truth, each one of you, with his neighbor for we are members of one another."

We are not advocating that you say everything you know to be true. You must consider the circumstances. There are times when it is better simply not to say anything at all. If, however, you choose to say something, make sure that it is true. We know one woman who has developed quite a reputation for fabricating things. People seem to sense that she is not a malicious liar because her heart indicates a basically sincere person. On the other hand, she simply makes something up when she does not know what the facts are. As this has become widely known, her credibility as a communicator has been nullified. People often don't believe her. Therefore, she is not the kind of person people listen to seriously.

B. Plan - Think About What You Are Going to Communicate.

Another woman had a terrible problem: she was always putting her foot in her mouth. She often would say something and then immediately regret it. But her spoken words could not be recalled. Even an apology cannot blot out the searing pain of an unfortunate remark. She was advised to hesitate for ten seconds between her thoughts and her responses. She also was encouraged to think about how it would sound to the person who was listening.

Proverbs 15:28 says, "The heart of the righteous ponders how to answer." Proverbs 15:2 says, "The mouth of fools spouts folly." Clearly, the Scriptures teach us to think before we communicate.

The following are some ways to ensure a well-planned communication:

1. Pray.
2. Establish the objective of your communication.
3. Know your audience.
4. Determine a relevant sequence of thoughts.
5. Determine relevant illustrations.
6. Determine the relevant vocabulary.
7. Make it clear what the other persons are supposed to know.
8. Determine the appropriate timing and amount of communication.

With this in mind, let's now examine each subpoint in greater detail.

1. PRAY.

There are many variables in any situation of give and take communication. Some of those variables relate to what is in your mind. You have certain thoughts on a subject and they form the context from which you are communicating. Your immediate tendency is to assume that is what other people are thinking as well, which often is not true. Other people have different contexts. They have specific needs and only a few of these may be apparent to us.

Since so many things are not subject to your knowledge at the time you communicate, you will want God's supernatural wisdom and guidance. That is why prayer is so important to all phases of communication.

Before Steve speaks to groups, he asks God to open people's hearts to what will be shared. Obviously, he cannot know all the different needs of the individuals in the group. So, he prays that God will use the things that are said to touch people in different ways. He often is amazed, after a talk, at how differently people have received and applied what he said.

2. ESTABLISH THE OBJECTIVE OF YOUR COMMUNICATION.

What are you trying to say? This applies equally to oral and written messages. If your goal is unclear to you, it will probably be unclear to other people. Write out your objectives ahead of time, if you can.

Dale Carnegie, undoubtedly the most famous teacher of effective public speaking in our time, declared that every talk (whether the speaker realizes it or not) has one of four major objectives: to make something clear, to impress and convince, to get action, or to entertain.[1]

3. KNOW YOUR AUDIENCE.

One of the real keys to effective communication is to know as much as possible about the people to whom you are communicating. They have needs. There are certain topics and presentation styles to which they respond and there are certain subjects and opinions to which they will not respond. (These are bear traps for the person who doesn't know his audience. Try to avoid them.)

If you appear to be sensitive to people's needs, if you use vocabulary and concepts they identify with, and if you avoid bear traps, you will have a much better chance of being effective in your communication.

4. DETERMINE A RELEVANT SEQUENCE OF THOUGHTS.

This is the basic content of what you are going to communicate. In light of your objectives and your audience, what would you like to say? If you have preparation time for major communications, you will find it helpful to keep a file of collected thoughts that occur to you over a period of time.

This is the point where you build logic into your communication. What specific things are necessary for that person to know in order for him to understand what you are trying to say? Start with the person's experience and current understanding of the subject. Move systematically to the added understanding you are trying to achieve. From time to time take a step back and put yourself in the other person's shoes. If you were listening to this, would you be informed or convinced?

You may find it helpful on this and on the next step to do your thinking in two parts: first draft, and detailed draft. At times it can be hard to keep the overall thread clear in your mind if you stop to think out details on your first pass through the content. It is better to keep a separate running check list of things you want to think about or improve upon later.

Press through the entire outline first, recording the thoughts that first occur to you and making entries on your separate check list. Then go back to fill in your outline by thinking more thoroughly, doing more research and asking for advice.

5. DETERMINE RELEVANT ILLUSTRATIONS.

Before He gave Himself full time to ministry, Jesus was a carpenter. Yet, He never once used a recorded term from that trade. Instead, he spoke in terms of crops and food and skies and flowers—all things that the people of His time and culture understood. Dale Carnegie points out, "Christ made the unknown clear by talking of it in terms of the known. He likened the kingdom of heaven to leaven, to nets cast into the sea, to merchants buying pearls. 'Go thou, and do likewise.'"[2]

Determine what would illustrate your communication to your audience. Generally you have to work with what is in their experience. With a young child, for example, you are probably going to have to work with something which can be found around the house.

Steve used to have great trouble recalling good, real-life illustrations for talks. Maybe you have had that problem. For him the best solution is to keep a small illustration notebook in his pocket. When he hears or sees a communicating story or humorous situation, he writes it down. Later, he reviews his collection when he prepares for his talks.

6. DETERMINE THE RELEVANT VOCABULARY.

If you are delivering a lecture to a group of scientists, you are able to use complex vocabulary. If you are talking to a grade school student, you are at another level altogether.

If we are not clear to everyone in our audience, we will have a "fog" problem in communication. Sometimes our attempts to communicate can be very amusing. For example, a story is told of a well-meaning Christian who decided to witness to a farmer he encountered along a country road.

Christian: "Are you a member of the Christian family?"

Farmer: "No, my name is Jones. But I think there is a family by the name of Christian down the road about a mile."

Christian: "No, no! You don't undertand what I mean. Are you lost?"

Farmer: "No, I've lived here all my life. We've owned this property for generations and I know my way around. I'm not lost."

Christian: "You still don't undertand. Are you prepared for the judgment day?"

Farmer: "Judgment day? When is it?"

Christian: "It could be today. It could be tomorrow. It could be any day."

Farmer: "Well, when you find out, let me know. I'm sure my wife and I will be happy to attend."

Remember, to keep your vocabulary relevant to your audience. Christians especially have to watch that they don't talk to non-Christians in "Christianese."

7. MAKE IT CLEAR WHAT THE OTHER PERSONS ARE SUP-POSED TO KNOW.

If you are seeking to convince a person of something, make sure he knows what it is. It is sometimes tempting not to do this. One very common problem in teaching people to sell is that they are reluctant to "close." They enjoy talking about the product and chatting with people in general, but when it comes time to ask for the sale the sellers feel uncomfortable. What some people don't realize is that most people appreciate knowing what you are driving at. Actually that helps them relax, knowing they can decide to say no or yes. Being more subtle can, at times, make people suspect our motive and intention.

8. DETERMINE THE APPROPRIATE TIMING AND AMOUNT OF COMMUNICATION.

Proverbs 15:23 declares, "A man has joy in an apt answer, and how delightful is a timely word!"

Proverbs 25:11 reads, "Like apples of gold in settings of silver is a word spoken in right circumstances."

Yes, timing is important, and so is the amount of communication we send.

Proverbs 13:3 says, "The one who guards his mouth preserves his life; the one who opens wide his lip comes to ruin."

Proverbs 10:19 (TLB) declares, "Don't talk so much. You keep putting your foot in your mouth. Be sensible and turn off the flow!"

There is a tremendous balance involved in deciding what to do when. There is no substitute for acquiring good judgment from the Lord and from personal experience. A good general piece of advice is to speak at just the right time, to keep working to improve your quality, and to be sure your quantity is not too great.

For example, Steve discovered this lesson while obtaining his graduate education in business administration at Harvard. As mentioned earlier, all the classes there were taught by the case-study method. As a result, a good share of the students' grades was determined on the basis of class participation. Some men took this as an invitation to make a comment on everything. They had high quantity, but were perceived by the students and professors alike as having low quality. As a result, overly vocal students did not get the best grades.

C. Motivate - Cause Your Audience to Be Motivated by, and Responsive to, Your Communication.

You can have the best content in the world on a subject, but if you are boring to listen to, you will not communicate well. All communication should aim to retain the interest of the listener or reader and cause him to take action after the communication is done. In a word this calls for "motivation."

We believe the following eleven actions will help to motivate your audiences:

1. Use humor.
2. Demonstrate interest.
3. Convey enthusiasm.
4. Encourage people.
5. Use change of pace.
6. Involve people.
7. Have a pleasant manner.
8. Touch natural motivations.
9. Use a "lead" or "hook."

10. End on a high note.
11. Seek feedback.

With this overview of our third major point, let's now examine each subpoint in greater detail.

1. USE HUMOR.

Dr. Howard Hendricks is a very effective speaker. Rarely does five to ten minutes go by in one of his talks without extensive laughter in response to what he is saying. He summarizes his feelings about humor by saying, "I open their mouths with laughter, and while they are open, I feed them a point."

An important point to remember is that people are both rational and emotional beings. It is difficult for us to simply clinically examine the logic of a matter and then be moved to action. Normally our emotions must be moved as well. There are many different ways to do this, and humor is one of the most effective.

Steve uses humor a lot even in his day-to-day informal conversation. "I find a meeting goes much better when people can laugh. It helps alleviate some of the possible tensions that arise in the course of a serious discussion. It also takes away the indecisive lethargy that can result in long meetings."

It is difficult to explain how to be humorous. One thing to realize is that humor generally results from something that has a touch of the ridiculous. Many circumstances have a little element of that naturally. Note what causes people to laugh. After a while, you begin to get a knack for seeing the humor in situations.

Another good technique for improving your use of humor is to read through joke books. Learn to observe what makes something funny.

In any case, cultivate your sense of humor. It is good for you and it is good in helping your audience to be more motivated and receptive to what you want to say and thus more motivated to action.

2. DEMONSTRATE INTEREST.

Our great tendency is to be interested in and excited about only those things which we are doing and which are natural for us. The key to motivation is to be able to put ourselves in the other person's shoes and get excited about what he is excited about.

Some time ago Steve was listening to someone promote attendance at an event. The approach was as follows, "Please come to this event. If you and everyone else will come, we have will 1000 people in attendance. We want to have 1000 people or more in attendance. Don't let us down. Be sure to come."

What is wrong with that approach to motivation? The main problem is that there is no reason given why a person should attend from that individual's point of view. It is obvious that it would meet the speaker's need if everybody would attend. The question is, though, "What would cause the person listening to decide to attend if he had not previously made the decision?" The answer is, "There probably has to be some benefit for *him* and not just for the *speaker*." Motivation should be *other-person* oriented. Too many of our attempts at motivation are "me" oriented, as opposed to "you" oriented.

Think back on experiences you have had involving the efforts of many people on a team. Did some people simply seem to be going along with what needed to be done? Did other people seem to really "own" the team's objective? This second category of people seemed to be willing to go the extra mile to make sure that an objective is accomplished. They seem to be "self-starters" in relation to the work on a project.

Generally, when you see this kind of ownership of the objectives, you are dealing with a person who has internalized the objectives and connected them intimately with things that are important to him. When this occurs, he can call on those tremendous inner reserves of energy and motivation. These reserves are not tapped in this way if he does not see how the objectives help him accomplish what he feels called to do.

3. CONVEY ENTHUSIASM.

Enthusiasm is contagious. If you are enthusiastic, the people around you will become enthusiastic. If you want to motivate people, be excited about what you are talking or writing about. In the best sense of the word, let your emotions *show*.

One time an American Christian speaker was delivering a message to a Mexican audience through an interpreter. As he spoke he made gestures that would be appropriate for an American audience. As his translator spoke, he made wider gestures, which were more communicative to the Mexican audience. (Mexicans tend to be more expressive with gestures than Americans.) As the talk went on, the speaker began to make noticeably wider gestures because of what the translator was doing. The humorous part of this was that the translator, of course, had to translate that into even wider gestures in order to convey the equivalent message to the Mexican audience. Eventually he almost had to turn cartwheels to convey the tremendous conviction expressed by the expansive gestures of the American speaker.

Enthusiasm of expression is contagious. Your enthusiasm will rub off on your audience.

Really examine yourself on this matter. Do you tend to be a negative person or perhaps one who expresses little emotion? If so, you are paying a great price in terms of the level of motivation that

people can read in listening to your communication. Try to think of some things about which you can be excited. Talk a little more about them and develop the habit of being enthusiastic.

4. ENCOURAGE PEOPLE.

Research has shown that it takes five to ten positive comments to compensate for one criticism or negative comment made to a person. This really highlights how important it is for us to encourage people at every opportunity. From time to time we may have to point out something which needs improvement. If we have not laid a basis of strong encouragement and positiveness, we may not be able to do this with effectiveness.

Think about the different people you know. Who are the ones you like to listen to? Don't you like to listen to those who encourage you? Don't you tend to avoid people who discourage you? If that is true of you, wouldn't it be true also of other people who listen to you?

Thinking of this point, Steve recalls what happened to him when he was in college. He was in a fraternity which was in a close race with another fraternity for the intramural sports trophy. In order to receive the trophy, Steve's fraternity would have to win the volleyball tournament. The previous year they had not even placed in the tournament. Obviously, they had a long way to go.

Steve took on the responsibility of organizing and leading the team. There were a number of men in the group who had been in varsity basketball during the winter season. Therefore, they had the height and basic coordination. The only problem was that they had the natural reactions of basketball players and not a lot of experience with volleyball. Basketball players catch the ball—which of course, is not appropriate for volleyball.

As a result, the team needed a lot of work. There was no obligation on anybody's part to do this. The main motivational tool Steve had available was encouragement. During the weeks before the competition. he spent time encouraging the various men selected for the team. One of the team members spent most of his time lounging around on the first floor of the fraternity house. He had good athletic potential, but he simply was not motivated. So Steve focused some extra attention on him.

The team won the intramural volleyball championship that year and, in turn, the fraternity won the athletic trophy. The formerly lazy fellow played a crucial role in their winning.

Ask yourself how you can be more encouraging to people. Do you respond negatively when new ideas are brought to your attention? As an act of faith and discipline, can you respond positively and with excitement as people propose things to you? As you do that, your communication will become more motivational to people.

5. USE CHANGE OF PACE.

This is particularly an issue when you are called upon to communicate at some length. An example of that would be a teaching situation. Be sure to schedule adequate breaks for people to stand up, stretch and maybe even get some refreshments. Vary the format of how you teach. Lecture a while and then go into discussion. Where possible, use skits or monologues. If possible, use visuals such as slides, films or overhead projection transparencies.

There is a natural tendency for people to get bored with one particular approach. As we vary approaches in our communication, we can refresh these people with a new point of interest. There is truth to the axiom that "variety is the spice of life."

6. INVOLVE PEOPLE.

Every once in a while as you are speaking, ask a question. It's good to see if people are following you. It also keeps them alert and motivated. When he teaches in his Sunday school class, Steve frequently uses small groups and other kinds of discussion formats to involve people. Oftentimes, early in the class time, he'll have one person turn to the next to discuss an item briefly. Frequently, they will have group discussions involving 10 or 12 people. After that, they further discuss the same questions as a larger group. The reason Steve does this is simple: "I can communicate more by involving them than I can by lecturing to them. My objective is not to occupy time in front of the class. My objective is to see concepts internalized."

7. HAVE A PLEASANT MANNER.

Proverbs 15:1 says, "A gentle answer turns away wrath, but a harsh word stirs up anger."

Proverbs 15:2 says, "The tongue of the wise makes knowledge acceptable."

Proverbs 15:4 reads, "A soothing tongue is a tree of life, but perversion in it crushes the spirit."

Proverbs 15:26 says, "Pleasant words are pure."

As you can see, your manner of communication can have a lot to do with your effectiveness. If your manner is gracious, you tend to cause a gracious response on the part of the person to whom you are communicating. If your manner is harsh, that person may respond in a harsh and opposing way.

8. TOUCH NATURAL MOTIVATIONS.

Dr. Ed Hill of Los Angeles, California, is an outstanding speaker. There are many reasons he is effective, but one of the prime factors is his use of human interest stories. Dr. Hill tells the story of how his mother sent him off to school with the words, "Ed, I am praying for you." When he got to school, he didn't even have enough money to register. But he stayed in line to register simply because he could hear the words of his mama, "Ed, I am praying for you." He got all the way to the front of the line (still without enough money to pay) when he felt a tap on the shoulder. He turned to see one of the university officials. He had been looking for Ed to tell him he had received a full four-year scholarship to attend the university, including some spending money. Dr. Hill said he could hear his mother's words again, "Ed, I am praying for you."

Once people have heard Dr. Hill tell that story personally, it is hard to even think of it without tears coming into their eyes. The reason: they all have mothers. Many people have mothers who prayed for them despite the fact that they often would disappoint their mothers. In this story, Dr. Hill touches on the rich ability that people have to identify with his experience.

9. USE A "LEAD" OR "HOOK."

This is another point that is particularly applicable when you are preparing longer communiques, such as lectures or articles. It is good to have some sort of hook or attention-getter at the beginning to gain people's interest in what you are about to say.

In Steve's Sunday school class, he often uses an interesting story or a joke he has heard that relates to the topic. Sometimes he uses a controversial or leading question on the subject. Notice in the chapters of this book that you find some form of lead at the beginning of each chapter.

One of the keys to motivating your listeners is to get off to a good start. A person who is motivated at the start is more likely to be motivated.

10. END ON A HIGH NOTE.

One of the main dividing lines between presentations which are effective and those which are not is the way in which they end. Some people seem to taper off into silence. Others end with real punch and effectiveness.

People tend to remember most what you say last. It is important for that to be what best summarizes and motivates. Some people even formalize this into suggesting that major talks ought to end with a "haymaker story," which emotionally and powerfully highlights your main point.·

If weak conclusions are one of your problems, start to think about how to strengthen them. Before you raise your hand to make a remark, think of how you are going to conclude it. If you cannot think of a particular story or clever saying, at least have the final few words down pat. Roll them over in your mind. See if they will be an effective summary of what you want to say. Proceed to make the rest of your comments and be sure you use your best conclusion.

11. SEEK FEEDBACK.

Up to this point, we have been suggesting various things you can do to be motivational in your communication. If you make use of feedback, you will be able to know how you are doing. As you talk to a person, or even an entire audience, you can usually sense how it is going. For example, indications of boredom, or at least distraction, include fidgeting, looking around, looking at watches, and yawning. Conversely, indications of a person's interest and motivation would be that person leaning forward in the chair, looking you straight in the eye, asking good questions, and smiling. If you sense people are responding positively, you're probably doing some of the right things.

If you sense that people are not responding well, you may need to implement more of the motivational techniques we've talked about. If it isn't clear to you how you are doing, you might try this simple method for gaining feedback: ask a question. One of the best questions to ask is whether or not people can paraphrase what you have been saying. You might try saying, "Does this make sense to you, Sam? How would you explain this? How do you see this as being helpful to you?" If you do this, you're not only gaining some feedback, you're also employing the motivational technique of involvement.

Some feedback is best received after your communication. If, for example, you have sent a written communication, it will only be possible for feedback to come after that has been read. One good way to get this feedback is from a survey. This is more appropriate in longer, more formal kinds of communication than in informal discussions.

For example, if a pastor wanted to know how he was communicating in his sermons, he would probably not get his best results by asking people about it as they leave on Sunday morning. There's a lot of social pressure, both from the pastor's presence and from those surrounding the pastor, to make a positive response, regardless of what the person really thinks of the sermon. If a pastor does want to know what listeners think, he ought to give them the chance to be anonymous and specific. A written survey is one way to accomplish this.

When you seek feedback you provide a real motivation to the people who are giving it. They realize that their opinions are important to you and that you want to hear what they think. You also have the opportunity to motivate yourself in the process. Things you are doing well will be encouraging to you. Those things that are indicated as not coming across well will motivate you to improve.

SUMMARY

There are many specific things we can do to improve our communication skills: (1) We can *be* more of the kind of person people listen to; (2) We can *plan* more concerning what we are going to communicate before we do it; and (3) We can *motivate* people who listen to us, or read what we have written, to be more interested in and responsive to our communication.

As with anything, practice makes perfect. The first and most obvious opportunities you will have to apply the lessons of this chapter will be in your informal conversation with people. Look back over the points in this chapter. See if you can find one or two that would now be particularly helpful in your conversations. For example, you may want to be more prayerful and thoughtful about responses to people before you speak or you may want to try to convey more enthusiasm.

These are improvements that you can seek to work on from day to day. When it is appropriate (such as in meetings), keep a pad of paper in front of you. Take notes and do little bits of mental preparation before you participate. As you contemplate opportunities to speak formally or to write at greater length, go back and make a more systematic application of the points of this chapter.

See if you can find some very good objective source of feedback and encouragement in your communication. Perhaps there is someone who hears you frequently and feels the freedom to be candid with you.

Keep learning from what you see and hear. Steve listens to and watches effective speakers with great interest. He not only is listening to *what* they say, but also to *how* they say it. He wants to discover what makes them effective. The same thing can be done with a magazine article. Ask yourself what made it effective. How can you seek to apply those same techniques in your writing?

Try to stretch yourself a little in this area. Schedule opportunities to do things beyond what you would normally encounter. For example, it is really good for Steve to have to teach in Sunday school. Among other things, it disciplines him to speak at least once a week. As he speaks, he is challenged to implement some improvements.

Think about and remember the following fact: Even if we make the most of our minds in every area other than what has been covered in this chapter, we still will greatly cripple our ability to influence and benefit other people with what God teaches us if we ignore these things.

— — —

I. PERSONAL APPLICATION

What is your highest personal priority application point found in the principles presented in this chapter? Enter that point in the indicated place in the Personal Application Worksheet at the end of the book. In the column next to that enter some specific plans to help you start implementing that point.

II. THOUGHT QUESTIONS

1. In a fair self-analysis, am I the kind of person to whom people listen? Why or why not?
2. What are my greatest natural strengths in communicating with others? Are there ways I can utilize these strengths better?
3. Do I think of my audience before I talk? Do I properly anticipate people's reactions to what I plan to say?
4. Do I agree or disagree with the statement: "A person needs to say what is on his mind?" Why?

III. ACTION PROJECT

Prepare and give a brief talk on a subject of concern to you and of interest to others. Use as many of the principles found in this chapter as you can. Obtain feedback from those who attended. Did you do a better job of communicating than usual?

IV. FURTHER STUDY MATERIALS

For more information on speaking and writing, you will want to consider the Further Study Materials for this chapter listed at the end of the book.

15

ESTABLISHING THE RIGHT BASIC RELATIONSHIP

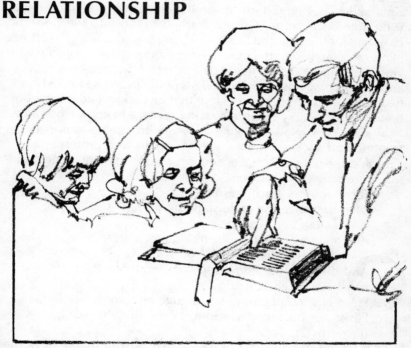

Sam (not his real name) grew up in a poor family, but he distinguished himself early in life. He made excellent grades in high school. His winning personality earned him many friends. He was a natural leader and was often elected by his peers to positions of responsibility. The pattern stayed the same when he went to college, when he served in the military, and when he started his first job. Then things began to change.

Sam started drinking; he fought with his wife; he had problems in his relationships at work. He was fired from his job; he divorced his first wife and married another. He had always had some prob-

lem about being nervous and getting frustrated easily, but the condition got worse. He changed jobs again, divorced his second wife,
married a third, and eventually divorced her as well. In his various
jobs, he had moments of brilliance, but they were substantially
dimmed by vast periods of average, or worse, performance.

You can see that Sam possessed some outstanding mental
capabilities. But he did not make the most of his talented mind.
Why not? Because he had not learned to tap into the powerful
resources for thinking and living which are available from God. Later
in his life Sam discovered how to have a personal relationship with
God. He began to return to the pattern which typified his early days
and which so obviously enhanced his potential. As he looked back,
he confessed to those close to him that he had wasted a great portion of his life, simply because he had not come to know God earlier.
Now God clearly was working in his life to enable him to begin
to cope and succeed mentally, emotionally and professionally.

Look at the offer God makes concerning discernment, understanding, knowledge and wisdom:

>For if you cry for discernment,
>Lift your voice for understanding;
>If you seek her as silver,
>And search for her as for hidden treasures;
>Then you will discern the fear of the Lord,
>And discover the knowledge of God.
>For the Lord gives wisdom;
>From His mouth come knowledge and understanding,
>He stores up sound wisdom for the upright. . .
>(Proverbs 2:3-7a).

In the biblical context, the following words normally have the
accompanying connotations: Discernment relates to discrimination,
judgment and interpretation. Understanding relates to comprehension. Knowledge relates to observation and memory. Wisdom relates
to the application of the other three in order to live life properly.

As you can see, these words encompass a rather large portion
of mental activity. In light of that, think of the significance of the
Proverbs 2 passage. If you have read this far, no doubt you desire
to have all four of those qualities in abundant measure: discernment, understanding, knowledge, and wisdom. And we have good
news for you: God gives them away to those who qualify.

"Well," you may say, "where do I stand in line?" That is what this chapter is all about: knowing and relating to God, and becoming eligible to receive these and the other mental capabilities. We must establish the right relationship because it is God who gives us the capability to make the most of our minds.

For example, often our minds do not function well because of our feelings about ourselves. If we feel there is no purpose in what we are doing, we lose motivation and don't operate at maximum effectiveness. If we don't feel loved by anyone we tend to feel mentally and emotionally "down," thus we function suboptimally. If we think we cannot do something, we probably will not do it, even if we could have. It is hard to imagine a purposeless, unloved, doubtful person making the most of his mind.

What is exciting is that knowing and relating personally to God helps us in each of these areas! God gives purpose and direction in life. We have His Word for it. "I will instruct you (says the Lord) and guide you along the best pathway for your life; I will advise you and watch your progress" (Psalm 32:8, TLB).

God makes us feel loved: "By this the love of God was manifested in us, that God has sent His only begotten Son into the world so that we might live through Him" (1 John 4:9). "And we have come to know and have believed the love which God has for us. God is love. . ." (1 John 4:16a).

God gives us confidence. Consider the example of Paul who declared, "I can do all things through Him who strengthens me" (Philippians 4:13). Also consider the example of Moses in Exodus 3 and 4. When God sought to commission Moses to lead the children of Israel out of Egypt, Moses was anything but confident. He said, "Please, Lord, I have never been eloquent, neither recently nor in times past, nor since Thou has spoken to Thy servant; for I am slow of speech and slow of tongue" (Exodus 4:10). Yet history records that God empowered and used Moses as a remarkable leader who displayed confidence in some seemingly impossible situations.

As we have seen in the previous chapters, God has given us many scriptural promises related to the mental area of life. As we trust God to fulfill these promises in our lives, He leads us to practical techniques. The main objective of this book is to show you ways to improve the use of your mind.

Therefore, we cannot complete the book without sharing with you the most crucial means by which to achieve that end. In order to experience all of the wonderful benefits God offers in the mental as well as other areas of your life, you must know Him personally and walk closely with Him.

The previous chapters have shown that God provides excellent ways in which people can make the most of their minds. But, unbelievable as it may seem, most people basically ignore His offer. Some people have yet to come to know Him personally. Even among those who have, most tap into His wisdom only on a token basis.

How to Walk with God

For many, perhaps, it is a matter of not knowing how to relate to God. In the remainder of this chapter, we would like to discuss four concepts that can strengthen your walk with God:
1. Being sure you are a Christian.
2. Experiencing God's love and forgiveness.
3. Being filled with the Spirit.
4. Walking in the Spirit.

This material is adapted from a series of Campus Crusade for Christ booklets called the *Transferable Concepts*, by Dr. Bill Bright, published by Here's Life Publishers.

1. BEING SURE YOU ARE A CHRISTIAN

The first of the spiritual prerequisites to managing yourself successfully is to be sure of your relationship with Christ. If you are not a Christian, you simply will not have access to the wisdom and guidance which God provides for those who believe in Him. And if you are not sure of your position in Christ, you will hesitate to entrust yourself to Him as you should to gain that wisdom and guidance.

What is involved in becoming a Christian? It involves agreeing with God concerning the fact that you have sinned (Romans 3:23) and that this sin separates you from God (Romans 6:23). It involves recognizing that Christ died in your place (Romans 5:8) and that you must invite Him to come into your life (Revelation 3:20) and ask Him to forgive you of your sins (Ephesians 1:7; 1 Corinthians 15:3). This bridges the chasm between you and God (John 14:6). If you have asked Christ into your life and are trusting in God's forgiveness through Christ, then you can know you are a Christian.

Trustworthiness of God and His Word

Foremost among the assurances that you are a Christian is the trustworthiness of God and His Word. Jesus said in Revelation 3:20, "Behold, I stand at the door and knock; if any one hears My voice and opens the door, I will come in to him . . ." Because of the perfect character of God, we can know without doubt that when He says He will do something, He will, in fact, do it. Therefore, if through an act of your will you sincerely opened the door of your heart to Christ, you can know that He has actually entered your life, for He would not deceive you.

The Presence of God in Our Lives

Now the trustworthiness of God and His Word is an external witness to the fact that you are a Christian. You also can sense God's presence in your life. We are told in 1 John 5:10 that "the one who believes in the Son of God has the witness *in himself* . . ." (emphasis ours).

One of the functions of God's Spirit in your life is to teach you the things of God, to illuminate them for you and to bring them to memory as needed. Have you ever been reading the Bible and had a certain thought you hadn't noticed before seem to jump out from the page and come to life? That is the work of the Holy Spirit in your life. Have you sensed that the Bible, has become more interesting and meaningful to you since becoming a Christian? Again, this is the doing of the Holy Spirit. Have you been constrained from doing something because, just as you were about to do it, a verse of Scripture suddenly came to mind and you realized that activity was wrong? Again, this is the work of the Holy Spirit in you. If these kinds of things are happening in your life, they testify to the fact that you are, indeed, a Christian.

If Christ has entered your life, you can also expect to see positive changes in your life—to the extent that you trust Him for these changes. It is God's purpose to conform us to the image of His Son (Romans 8:29) and that involves changes for all of us.

After we became Christians, and particularly after we learned to trust God moment by moment, our lives began to change, sometimes in ways that we hadn't even anticipated. Our thoughts began to change; many of our actions changed. And we had an increasing desire to obey and to please God. You should be experiencing some of these kinds of things in your own life. You can, of course, refuse to trust God to implement changes in your life. If you do refuse, as a Christian, you will find yourself very frustrated and unhappy. And this, too, is a testimony of God's presence in your life.

You Can Become A Christian

It may be that, as you have been reading about how to become a Christian and how to be assured of your relationship with God, you have realized that you are not a Christian. You can receive Jesus Christ into your life right now by simply acknowledging the fact that there is sin in your life which needs to be forgiven and by asking Him to enter your life and to make you what He wants you to be. "But *as many as received Him*, to them He gave the right to become children of God, even to those who believe in His name" (John 1:12, emphasis ours).

The following is a suggested prayer: "Lord Jesus, I need You. I open the door of my life and receive You as my Savior and Lord. Thank You for forgiving my sins. Take control of my life. Make me the kind of person You want me to be."

If this prayer expresses your desire, pray it now and ask Christ to come into your life and establish your relationship with God.

If you just prayed that prayer, reread this section on Being Sure You Are a Christian before you go on. Write Campus Crusade for Christ, San Bernardino, CA, 92414, for further help and information.

2. EXPERIENCING GOD'S LOVE AND FORGIVENESS

When you became a Christian, you entered into a father-child type of relationship with God (John 1:12). You also gained a chance for close fellowship with Him. As a Christian, you can talk with God directly and receive His directions concerning the pathway that is best for you (Psalms 32:8).

When you sin, your *relationship* with God is not broken. You don't cease to be God's spiritual child any more than you cease to be your human parents' child when you do something they don't like.

However, your close *fellowship* with God is disrupted when you sin. In 1 John 1 the word used to describe fellowship with God in the original language means "to share in common." When we sin, we cease to live in a way that is totally "shared in common" with

God (1 John 1:5,6). We are not anxious to talk to God because we feel guilty and embarrassed by our sin. Our fellowship with Him has grown cold.

Confession Is the Solution

Fortunately, God anticipated that we probably would sin (1 John 2:1) and He provided a way for us to experience His forgiveness and to be restored to close fellowship with Him. We see in 1 John 1:9, "If we confess our sins, He is faithful and righteous to forgive us our sins and to cleanse us from all unrighteousness." The word for "confess" in the original language means to "speak the same thing" or to "agree with." If sin illustrates that we are out of agreement (not in common) with God on a matter, we then must come back into agreement with God to restore the fellowship.

Whereas your guilty feelings over sin tend to make you not want to talk to God, you must talk to Him to experience His love and forgiveness. When you confront God "face to face" with what you have done, agreeing with Him that it is wrong, and repenting of your wrong action or attitude, then you open the floodgates of God's love and forgiveness which pour into your heart. This is a forgiveness you usually can *feel* — as a sense of relief and well-being — as well as something you can know intellectually on the basis of God's promise. This confession of a sin includes a genuine regret for having committed it and a sincere desire to refrain from doing it again. Simply acknowledging that something is a sin with the full intention of repeating it doesn't bring the flood of forgiveness.

Take Care of Your Sins

Perhaps you have been a Christian for some time, but God does not seem to be working in your life. It could well be that some unconfessed sins have put up a barrier between you and God and have cut short His efforts on your behalf.

If that is the case, why not take care of it right now? First, ask God to reveal to you sins you have not confessed to Him. Write all of them on a sheet of paper. Don't be introspective; just jot down the sins that God brings to your mind. When you have completed your list, write across it God's promise in 1 John 1:9: "If we confess our sins, He is faithful and righteous to forgive us our sins and to cleanse us from all unrighteousness."

Now, if you agree with God that the things you have listed are sin, and if you are truly sorry for your wrong actions or thoughts, and if you honestly say to God that, though you are weak and might do the things again, it is your genuine desire not to do them, then you can thank Him for forgiving your sins on the basis of Christ's death for them.

Ask God to guide you in seeking any necessary forgiveness from other persons concerning these sins. Then, destroy your list, knowing that you are forgiven.

3. BEING FILLED WITH THE SPIRIT

Can you relate to the plight of the apostle Paul? Here is his problem: "No matter which way I turn I can't make myself do right. I want to but I can't. When I want to do good, I don't; and when I try not to do wrong, I do it anyway. . . .It seems to be a fact of life that when I want to do what is right, I inevitably do what is wrong" (excerpted from Romans 7:18-21, TLB).

Not in Our Own Strength

In Romans 8, Paul states that man was never intended to live the Christian life in his own strength. Even the best-intentioned and most highly disciplined among us will eventually give in to temptation and fall short of the mark. Our old sinful nature will thwart our good intentions.

If that is the case, then why does God hold up to us standards that are impossible to meet? The answer lies in the fact that God doesn't want us to live the Christian life at all; *He* wants to live the Christian life in us and through us.

To understand this concept, let's back up a moment to whenever it was that you became a Christian. When you received Christ into your life, you actually received God's Spirit also (Ephesians 1:13, 14; Colossians 2:9,10). The Holy Spirit has all of the resources that are needed to live the Christian life: the power, the wisdom, the constant availability.

Now *that* is the power source which God wants us to draw on as we seek to live the Christian life. In fact, in Ephesians 5:18, God actually commands us to be "filled with the Holy Spirit"; that is to say, we are commanded to be directed and empowered by the Holy Spirit.

Two Types of Christians

In 1 Corinthians 2:15 – 3:3 we learn that a Christian can be in one of two states: spiritual or carnal (man of flesh). In Campus Cruade for Christ, we like to illustrate these two possibilities with the following circles:

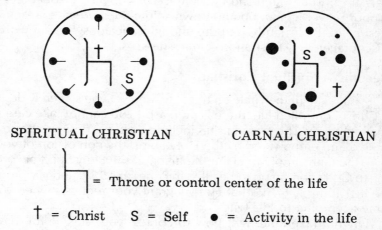

SPIRITUAL CHRISTIAN   CARNAL CHRISTIAN

= Throne or control center of the life

† = Christ   S = Self   ● = Activity in the life

The circles represent the lives of the two types of Christians. Each person has received Christ, as indicated by the respective crosses inside the circles. The spiritual Christian has put Christ on the throne of his life — he is allowing Christ to run his life as he is directed and empowered by the Holy Spirit.

The carnal Christian has placed himself on the throne of his life — he is running his life by himself without the benefit of God's direction and power. Notice that in the life of the spiritual Christian, the activities, as represented by the dots, are in balance. This represents the peace, joy, and purpose enjoyed by a person in harmony with God's plan. The interests of the carnal Christian are in disarray, representing the discord and frustration resulting from not being in harmony with God's plan.

Now, which of these circles represents your life? Is it the circle on the left? Some of the characteristics and actions of the spiritual Christian show that he is Christ-centered and empowered by the Holy Spirit; he introduces others to Christ; he has an effective prayer life; he has an understanding of God's Word; he is able to trust God and to obey Him; he increasingly is able to exhibit the fruit of the

Spirit in his life as he matures and trusts Christ to develop this fruit in him. The fruit, as recorded in Galatians 5:22,23, includes love, joy, peace, patience, kindness, goodness, faithfulness, gentleness and self-control.

Or is your life best represented by the circle on the right? The carnal Christian often shows evidence of unbelief, disobedience, a poor prayer life, an up-and-down spiritual experience, a lack of desire for Bible study, impure thoughts, jealousy, guilt, worry, discouragement, frustration, aimlessness.

Become A Spiritual Christian

If you relate to the circle on the right, and yet you sincerely desire a Christ-controlled life, there is no reason you cannot take care of that right now. The prerequisites include a sincere desire to be controlled and empowered by the Holy Spirit, the confession of your sins, the faith simply to claim the filling of the Holy Spirit according to God's command to be filled in Ephesians 5:18, and His promise in 1 John 5: 14, 15 that He will grant your requests when you pray according to His will.

Why not take time right now to confess your sins, if you have not already done so, and to ask God to take control of the throne of your life? Ask Him to fill you with the Holy Spirit in accordance with His command, and *know* that He will do so because your request is made in accordance with His will. Your authority is the trustworthiness of God and His Word.

Finally, thank God for filling you with His Spirit as He promised to do, and then get on with the business of living, trusting God to lead you along the pathway He knows is best for you, trusting Him to conform you increasingly to the image of His Son and trusting Him to provide the power to live as He wants you to live.

4. WALKING IN THE SPIRIT

Now the question is, If Christ is on the throne of your life and you are being controlled and empowered by the Holy Spirit, is it possible for you to sin, thereby disrupting your fellowship with God? The answer is "yes," because, even though you have yielded the control of your life to Christ, your ego is still very much alive. You still have freedom of choice. You can disregard Christ's control and do what *you* want to do at any time.

When you *do* disregard Christ's direction, your sin is really twofold; first, you are removing Christ from His position of leadership in your life and second, you are committing whatever else it is that is contrary to His will.

Be Continually Filled

Unlike the indwelling of the Spirit then, which occurs when you become a Christian, the filling of the Spirit is not a one-time, irrevocable occurrence. In God's command in Ephesians 5:18, the verb used in the original Greek for the filling of the Spirit means to be *constantly* and *continually* filled. Therefore, when you remove Christ from the throne of your life through sin, it is both possible and necessary to restore Him to His rightful position by being filled with the Spirit again.

This new filling takes place in the same way as before. You confess your sin to God, agreeing with Him that it is wrong, and experience His forgiveness on the basis of Christ's sacrifice nearly 2,000 years ago. Remember that confession involves repentance—a genuine remorse for having committed the wrongdoing and a desire to avoid a repeat performance. You then again surrender the control of your life to Christ and appropriate the Holy Spirit (by faith in accordance with God's command) to be filled and His promise to grant any requests made in accordance with His will.

Spiritual Breathing

This process could be described as "spiritual breathing." When you breathe physically, you exhale the impure air and you inhale the pure. When you breathe spiritually you "exhale" through the confession of your sin, and you "inhale" by appropriating the fullness of the Holy Spirit by faith.

This is an ongoing process, one to be repeated whenever sin occurs in your life. The more mature Christian may only need to breathe spiritually occasionally, whereas the newer Christian may find that He must repeat the process often. However, if that new Christian sees to it that he is continually Spirit filled, God will be free to work in his life for good, bringing him to maturity.

In fact, as you walk with God, breathing spiritually as needed, you can expect the following types of things to be true of your life: You will demonstrate more and more of the fruit of the Spirit (Galatians 5:22, 23) and be increasingly conformed to the image of Christ (Romans 12:2; 2 Corinthians 3:18). Your prayer life and the study of God's Word will become more meaningful; you will experience God's power in witnessing (Acts 1:8); you will be prepared for spiritual conflict against the world (1 John 2:15-17), and against the flesh (Galatians 5:16, 17) and against Satan (1 Peter 5:7-9; Ephesians 6:10-13); and you will increasingly experience God's power to resist temptation and sin (1 Corinthians 10:13; Philippians 4:13; Ephesians 1:19-23; 6:10; 2 Timothy 1:7; Romans 6:1-16). In short, you will be equipped to make the most of your mind and your life in a way you never before dreamed possible.

— — —

I. PERSONAL APPLICATION

What is your highest personal priority application point found in the principles presented in this chapter? Enter that point in the indicated place in the Personal Application Worksheet at the end of the book. In the column next to that enter some specific plans to help you start implementing that point.

II. THOUGHT QUESTIONS

1. How·does a close walk with God benefit me in making the most of my mind?
2. Would it be fair to say that I confess my sins to God and turn from them quickly?
3. Am I filled with the Spirit most of the time? If not, what can I do to improve?
4. What are my top three specific prayer requests for my spiritual growth? With whom can I share these for prayer support?

III. ACTION PROJECT

Memorize the following verses of Scripture: 1 John 1:9; Ephesians 5:18; and 1 John 5:14,15. Recite them to yourself several times a day for at least a week. As you do that, ask if you are applying them in your daily life.

IV. FURTHER STUDY MATERIALS

For more information on establishing the right basic relationship, you will want to consider the Further Study Materials for this chapter listed at the end of the book.

16

MAKING
THESE CONCEPTS
YOURS

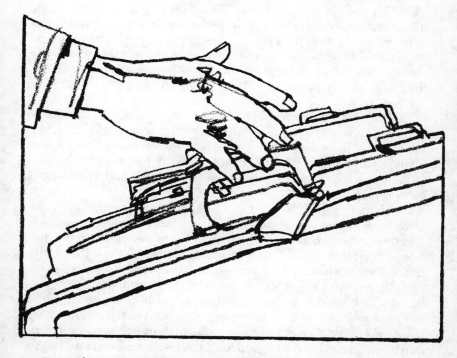

Recently, Steve was asked to develop some ideas for a resource-center project for the ministry of Campus Crusade. The need for this had been a burden on his heart for some time. When he received the assignment he consciously prayed and committed himself to start thinking about it. He sought advice from his colleagues and shared some of his thoughts with them. He pulled together a report of progress in the area and formally presented that several times. He continued to pray that God would give His wisdom to the project.

After a few weeks, he found ideas were beginning to pop into his head on the project. He wrote them down and put them together in his resource center file. Often, when he would awaken at night, he would be thinking about several ideas related to the center. He would write them down. One night he filled an entire page with ideas.

Finally, he pulled out his file of ideas, prayed and began to review them and organize the thoughts into a total plan. Very quickly he found himself thinking thoughts almost faster than he could write them down. Ten pages were filled with notes in less than two hours time. When he had to leave the project and go to a meeting on another subject, he found he continued to have ideas. He wrote them down even while he was in the other meeting. Eventually, the entire center plan took shape. It was to have fifteen different sections to it.

That same night he was out caroling with a group and became chilled. He went home early and found he was a little sick. Yet, when the chill awakened him at 12:30 a.m., he found several new ideas occurring to him. In the next hour, hunched over the kitchen table, he wrote several pages of overview notes and vision ideas for the plan.

We share this incident with you simply to say, it works! What we have been telling you about in this book works. Steve prayed and asked for wisdom; he committed himself to concentrate on this; he received information from various sources; he organized some of the information he received preliminarily and presented parts of it; he received feedback; he allowed his information to simmer in his subconscious for an extended period of time; he captured bursts of insight that God gave periodically. When the time came to put everything together, his mind was thoroughly prepared for maximum creativity and productivity. When he prayed and began the plan, he reaped the benefits.

You can make the most of your mind, too. We have shared some life-changing concepts with you. If you apply them, they will work for you.

The freshman orientation speaker at the Massachusetts Institute of Technology once said, "Getting an education at MIT is like trying to take a drink from a fire hose." Perhaps you feel a little like that after having received all the information and challenges in this book. To help you swallow and digest it all, we would like to review a little and explain things in a somewhat different way.

You may recall that the objectives of this book were to help you learn:

1. How to become motivated to use your mind most effectively.
2. How God can relate to your mind and cause you to make the most of it.
3. How to use simple, specific and practical ways in which you can improve your mental skills.
4. How to apply what you learn to your daily life.

Motivation

Let's look back at the book in light of these objectives. Let's look at the first objective, motivation. Chapter 1, "Getting Started," was offered mainly to help you start to want to make the most of your mind. It documented the great potential we have in our minds and pointed out that most people do not realize their mental potential. In that chapter you read about people who, by God's grace, rose above the norm.

Susbsequent chapters began with a story which illustrated the need we all have for the concepts which were to be presented in the chapter. Next, you were given scriptural and other reasons for implementing these concepts in your life. At the end of each chapter there were thought questions. Part of the reason for including them was to give you one more opportunity to consider why you should know and implement the concepts presented.

People do what they want to do. We want you to have a burning desire to make the most of your mind.

God's Role

Second, we want you to see how crucially important it is for you to walk with God if you want to function at your mental peak. God is supernatural. God wants to interact with us and teach us. We literally would be foolish to turn down His help.

Throughout the book, there have been frequent references to God and to how He alleviates anxiety, gives proper mental attitudes, answers prayers for wisdom, instructs us through His Word and helps us to observe, interpret, organize, and listen. The Scriptures are quoted often. At many points you have been encouraged to pray and ask God for some specific form of wisdom.

Unfortunately, many people don't know how to establish and cultivate a close relationship with God. So, we included Chapter 15, "Establishing the Right Basic Relationship."

From our perspective, we can do your mind no better favor than to help you draw closer to God.

Simple, Specific and Practical Techniques

Most of this book is dedicated to showing you how to make the most of your mind. We have sought to give you concepts that you can use today, right where you are. We have learned most of what is presented not from books, but from life. We and many others use these ideas and know they work. You just need to start using them in whatever you do.

Suppose, for example, you are a student. You must read and listen well because your success as a student hinges on how well you absorb information. If you don't know how to "speed-read" you really ought to learn right away. If you don't know how to dig in and study written material, go back to Chapter 9 and apply the techniques taught there. If you don't listen aggressively, go back to Chapter 8 and learn how to lean forward, focus and take good notes.

What about remembering? How well do you do on exams? Do you forget key facts? Remember DOARS? Apply it when you study for your next exam.

What about observing, interpreting, being creative, solving problems, speaking, and writing? If you want to be a good student, you need to do them all well.

What if you are a homemaker with two small children at home? "Surely," you say, "I can't use this when all I do all day long is talk 'baby talk'." Don't bail out quite so fast. Without mental stimulation, you will shrink mentally. If that doesn't bother you, fine.

If it does bother you, reverse the trend. Buy a tape recorder and start to saturate your mind daily with tapes of the Scriptures and of specific information on topics of interest to you. Play the tapes over five to ten times to secure the concepts in your mind. Practice good listening techniques as much as you can. Use the memory techniques to retain the key points in your mind in an accessible way. Discuss what you are learning with other people. Seek to apply at least one point from every tape. In summary, find a way to grow mentally despite the limitations of your circumstances.

Also, seek to apply and teach these concepts to your children. Your young children are already learning at a far greater rate than you are learning, but you can help them to learn even faster. Is your child good at "scanning," for example? Sometimes children will focus and explore well, but miss the big picture.

What about problem solving? Well, a child probably won't use the charts anytime soon, but he might be able to improve in the area of identifying the cause of problems.

What about being creative? Any parents we have ever met have wanted their children to be creative. Yet, often for reasons of convenience, parents establish needlessly narrow boundaries for their children's behavior. For example, one time Steve's daughter, Debbie, was playing with her mother's emery board. She asked if she could eat ice cream with it. At first her mother told her, "No!" But, on thinking about it, she complimented Debbie for being creative. Debbie's "pushing of a conventional boundary" was far more significant than the inconvenience of cleaning off the emery board.

Or, suppose you are a truck driver or a farmer or a production line worker? Sometimes you may find mental "dead spots" in your job. You have to stay alert, but it doesn't take your total focus. Redeem those times with praying, listening to Scriptures and other worthwhile tapes. Plan future projects and keep a note pad handy to record your thoughts. Select a list of fruitful discussion topics that could benefit both you and your partner and talk about them instead of always letting the conversation drift.

Set some specific objectives for development in the mental area of your life. For example, do you want to remember names better? Go back and apply the content of Chapter 8 or buy and study one of the recommended books on memory development. Learn the principles at home or on breaks, then work on application during the "dead spots." Consider memorizing Scripture this way.

Look over the techniques taught on creativity and see if you can find some way to improve the techniques you use on your job. You may even get a raise.

What if you are an executive? What if you are a retired person? What if you live alone? What if there are many people at home in your family? No matter what your circumstance, you can seek to make the most of your mind! Every situation has liabilities and assets. Find ways to keep from being mentally disabled by the liabilities and learn to take full advantage of the assets. Let that be your first problem-solving assignment.

For example, if you are an executive, you have many natural opportunities to make decisions and to learn to cope with anxiety. If you are retired, you have time and may need to seek mental challenges. If you live alone, you may have time but not constant mental stimulation from others and opportunity to discuss concepts with others. If you live with a big family you have the opposite pluses and minuses.

Whatever your circumstances, make the most of your mind!

Right Attitudes and Good Skills

As you can see from the above, we had you in mind when we wrote this book—regardless of your circumstance. What is more, we focused on only the attitudes and skills which you will need every day. Most people, for example, worry from time to time. That consumes mental (as well as emotional and physical) energy. It distracts from the capability to focus the mind. The negative attitudes which often are associated with anxiety can severely disable our constructive creativity. Therefore we included a chapter in the book on how to handle anxiety.

Most adults close their minds to new ideas. They stop asking good, knowledge-building questions. They often lack internal motivation and discipline to pursue a thought to full comprehension and application. So, we included a chapter on maintaining the right mental attitudes.

How many minutes into the day can you go before you make your first observation? Not even one! The minute you awaken you consciously begin to listen and, when you open your eyes, to see. It is not a question of *whether* you observe, but rather *how well* you observe.

Similarly, you can't go far in the morning without making a decision: what to wear, what to say, or whether to see if the newspaper has arrived yet. These decisions may all be very easy. But most days contain opportunities to make more significant, harder decisions which can benefit from at least a reflective moment of prayer and thought and possibly from a simple pass through the decison-making process.

What vacation, work project, committee assignment, or meeting doesn't warrant at least a simple plan? What letter, phone call, counseling opportunity, brief talk or memo doesn't warrant at least quick recollection of some of the principles of effective speaking and writing?

What newspaper, magazine article or book can't become more useful to you if you apply the principles of reading better? What conversation, sermon or seminar can't benefit you more, if you listen better?

The point is that you have chances every day — probably every waking hour of the day — to be helped by the principles taught in this book.

Receiving, Processing and Sending

To remember and understand better the many skills you have learned, think of them as being in one of three categories: receiving, processing, and sending.

When we are taking information into our minds we are "receiving." When we are observing, listening, reading, and studying, we are "receiving" (for the most part).

"Processing" is what the mind does with the information it receives. This is the central function of the mind. This is what we might call "thinking." Interpreting, organizing, being creative, planning, solving problems, making decisions, remembering and forgetting are basically "processing" functions. Of course, all of the other functions involve some "processing" as well.

"Sending" is where we get a chance to influence the world around us. Here is where we unload on others some of the precious cargo of our thoughts. Speaking and writing are the skills we shared with you to improve your "sending."

Making Your Personal Application Worksheet Work for You

The fourth objective of this book was to show you how to apply what you have learned. At the end of each chapter there are a number of features to help you make these concepts yours. For example, you have been encouraged at the end of each chapter to fill out a portion of the Personal Application Worksheet. As you have been faithfully doing this, you may have wondered where you would ever get the time to carry out all these wonderful intentions. At this point we are going to grapple with the realities of fitting these things in.

The fact is that you probably cannot immediately implement all of your plans in the right-hand column of your worksheet. What can you do? You can at least start on one thing.

Look over all of your entries of priority points from each chapter, in the large left-hand column. If you could only improve in one area right now, which one would it be? Compare the different application points and determine the one which you feel you need the most. To the left of that point put the number "1"— in the small column entitled Final Priority Rating at the extreme left of the page.

Now, mentally separate your number one choice from the rest of the list and ask the same questions (above) of the remaining points. In the Final Priority Rating column to the left of your choice, put the number "2."

Go through the same process again and select a number "3" choice.

Now look over your "specific plans" to the right of your top three choices. Can you imagine yourself implementing these plans? Are they within your means? Can you immediately start with the first step of your plans? If you answered yes to these questions, put a number "1" to the left of the first step of your plan. If your plan isn't in sequenced steps, put a number "1" to the left of the best single step for you to start with. Go through this for each of your top three choices and circle each of those number "1's" so they will be clearly visible among the other items in the plan.

Next, either tear your Personal Application Worksheets out of the book or write the three top priority personal application points and their corresponding top priority action steps on a 3" x 5" card. Attach the one or the other to a place where you will see it every morning—first thing.

Every morning when you see your reminder list, pray for the implementation of the top three points in your life. Then ask yourself the following question: "Is there some way that I can spend a minimum of five minutes implementing the top action step on my number one priority application point?" If the answer is "yes," put it in your schedule.

Next ask, "Is there also some way I can spend a minimum of five minutes implementing my top action step on my number three priority personal application point?" If the answer is "yes," put that in your schedule too.

Next ask, "Is there also some way I can spend a minimum of five minutes implementing my top action step on my number three priority personal application point?" If the answer is "yes," put that in your schedule too.

If there is a way to do all three, that is great. If there is only time to work toward two, that's also great. If there is only time to work on your number one priority mental development project, that's fine. If you have limited time, at least try to make progress on the one item that is most important to you.

If you consistently can't find the time to spend even five minutes daily on even just your number one priority, then you are not really serious about making the most of your mind. Pray and ask God for more motivation and more creativity in working it into your schedule.

In any case, solicit a prayer partner who can talk with you about your mental improvement project(s) and who can follow up on you as well as pray for you. Keep him or her posted on how you are doing.

Making a Habit of Building Your Mind

There are a number of things you can do to make your mental development a habit.

First, when you achieve substantial progress in one of the three areas of needed improvement, you will want to start focusing on a new area in its place. Look back over your Personal Application Worksheet. Select the next highest priority application point in the manner outlined above. Seek to implement it as one of your *current* top three action steps toward making the most of your mind.

Second, as you might guess, it is hard to start and keep at any new project. If you have this problem read back over Chapter 3, especially under "Motivation" and "Discipline/Persistence." Apply some of the concepts presented there. For example, pray and ask God for His motivation and discipline. Remember why it is important to you to do this. Find ways to make it fun. Associate with other people who are enthusiastic about what you are trying to do.

Keep your action steps easy to implement and broken down into little bite-sized pieces. When you get a little five-minute break between job assignments, home projects, or television programs, take a little "mental development" break by spending a few minutes on your improvement project. When all else fails, just "force" yourself to start, by promising that you absolutely will quit in five minutes.

Over the long haul there is no substitute for your personal internal motivation to make the most of your mind. If you want to, you will find a way. So keep reviewing the motivation sections of this book (e.g., Chapter 1) and the particular reason you want to improve. Place graphic reminders around where you will see them frequently. Talk about it with other people. As you act interested and excited, you will begin to feel enthusiastic.

Third, feed your mind with at least as much care as you feed your body. You would never knowingly poison your body; yet, you could easily be poisoning your mind every day. Evaluate what you watch on television, for example. Is it contributing to your mental development or detracting from it? If it is detracting, turn the program off and go read a good book or engage in a good conversation with a friend or family member. Try out some of the principles of reading or listening better as you do. This may be your best source of time for mental development.

Fourth, learn to capitalize on your mental strengths. Perhaps you naturally have a good memory. By using the techniques presented in this book and those taught in the recommended reading material, refine and enhance your natural strength. As a matter of good stewardship of a gift from God, use what He has given you to memorize Scripture. Teach others how to improve their memories. Become involved in other activities which can benefit from your skill.

It builds confidence in you as you trust God and succeed at something. It benefits others. And, by the way, that is the way God intended it to be. No one person possesses all strengths. We all need to benefit from some of the strengths of others and to minister to others in areas where we are strong.

Perhaps the whole mental area of life is fairly strong in you. If so, consider teaching the content of this book in a home study group, Sunday school class or lunch-hour discussion group at work.

THE CHOICE IS YOURS

Since you have read to this point, obviously you have a serious interest in making the most of your mind. We are excited for you and with you. In this book we have shared with you all we felt we could fruitfully say to you in a book on the subject. We have structured the book to stimulate your motivation, thoughts, and actions.

So, when you close the pages of this book the choice will be yours. Will you allow the great power and wisdom of God to permeate and enlighten your mind? Will you seek to dispense with anxiety and maintain positive, helpful mental attitudes? Will you keep using and improving your key mental skills?

If you will, by God's grace, you will soar to mental heights beyond what you even thought you could. The choice is yours. Will you?

— — —

I. PERSONAL APPLICATION

Has the content in this chapter stimulated you to think of other application points that you want to consider for future action? If so, enter them in your Personal Application Worksheet in the row marked for this chapter.

II. THOUGHT QUESTIONS

1. How would I rate myself on a scale from 1 to 10 in my general performance in each of the following three categories of mental activity:
   a. Spiritual (walk with God)?
   b. Attitudes?
   c. Skills?
2. How would I rate myself on a scale from 1 to 10 in my general performance in each of the following three categories of mental skill:
   a. Receiving?.
   b. Processing?
   c. Sending?
3. Do my answers to questions 1 and 2 above give me any new overall insights on where I should focus my mental development efforts?
4. What else can I do to motivate myself to pray and work harder toward making the most of my mind?

III. ACTION PROJECT

Start on your top action step of your number one priority application point, right now.

IV. FURTHER STUDY MATERIALS

For more information on making these concepts yours, you will want to consider the Further Study Materials for this chapter listed at the end of the book.

PERSONAL APPLICATION
WORKSHEET

These sheets are provided to help you apply what you are learning in this book. At the end of each chapter you are asked to pause and write your number one priority point to apply from that chapter. Enter that point in the left column while the chapter is still fresh in your mind.

You are also asked at the end of each chapter to enter in the right column a few thoughts as to how you will get started in implementing each point in your life. The best time to think about this is also right after you finish reading the chapter.

This takes only a moment before you move into the next chapter, and it greatly increases the chances that you will do something with what you learn. Take the time. You are the one who will benefit.

At the end of the last chapter you are instructed to set priorities among this list of application points and plans. It will probably be impossible for you to start on all of the points at once. Therefore, select the most important one(s) and start on it (them) first.

Feel free to photocopy this blank worksheet for use by yourself and by others.

Final Priority Rating	Number One Priority Application Point from Each Chapter	Specific Plans To Start Implementing Each Point In My Life
	I. Getting Started:	
	II. Handling Anxiety and Guilt:	
	III. Maintaining the Right Mental Attitudes:	